# Praise for *Confessions of a Public Speaker*

"A fresh, fun, memorable take on the most critical thing: what we say. Highly recommended."

*—Chris Anderson, Editor-in-Chief,* Wired

"Scott Berkun tells it like it is. Whether you're speaking to 10 people or 1,000, you will gain insights to take your skills to the next level. It's a rare book that will make you think *and* laugh."

*—Tony Hsieh, CEO, Zappos.com*

"Smart, funny, and provocative, Scott Berkun's *Confessions of a Public Speaker* puts a very modern and wholly relevant spin on the fine art of public speaking."

*—Suzy Welch, bestselling author and public speaker*

"Your next talk will be 10 times better if you read this book first. Using wit and years of experience, Berkun takes a thoughtful look at the art of public speaking and teaches you how to inspire, educate, and motivate the next time you step on stage."

*—Gina Trapani, founding editor of Lifehacker.com*

"Loved it! This is a very informative and entertaining look at the important art of public speaking. Anyone who speaks for a living— including teachers—will greatly benefit from this book."

*—Garr Reynolds, author of* Presentation Zen
*(New Riders Press)*

"What a relief to finally read a book that prepares a presenter for the stage beyond eye contact and gestures. Scott covers a breadth of practical and humorous insights from his own success and mistakes."

*—Nancy Duarte, CEO of Duarte, Inc.; author of*
Slide:ology *(O'Reilly)*

"Part of me wishes that Scott Berkun had never written this book.... Scott is giving everyone a peek behind the curtain...what will we do now that [he] has revealed our secrets?... It's a great read and full of practical tips on presenting. I recommend it highly."

*—John Baldoni, author of* Great Communication
Secrets of Great Leaders *(McGraw-Hill)*

"Fun, funny, useful, easy to read, practical. I learned something from every chapter, and even when I knew the point Scott was trying to make, I still benefited from his framing and personal anecdotes."

—Bradley Horowitz, VP of Product Management, Google

"Cicero said you should make your audience receptive, attentive, and trusting. How do you do that? First, avoid pretentious references to dead people. Second, read Scott Berkun's fun and useful guide to public speaking."

—Jay Heinrichs, author of Thank You for Arguing (Three Rivers Press)

"Confessions of a Public Speaker is fresh, honest, comprehensive, and well organized. The suggestions [Scott] offers are GOLD for anyone who has to deliver a presentation."

—Susan RoAne, keynote speaker and author of How to Work a Room (Harper)

"Packed with invaluable tips and advice—gold dust for anyone who ever has to talk to a crowd. If only there was a way I could send a copy to myself 10 years ago!"

—Tom Standage, business editor for the Economist; author of A History of the World in 6 Glasses (Walker Publishing Company)

"An easy-to-read and easy-to-apply set of actions anyone can take to get and keep the attention of the audience.... Read this book. Put into practice what you have read, and it's sure to make you as comfortable [speaking] to groups as [you are when chatting] with friends."

—Arthur R. Pell, PhD, editor and updater of Dale Carnegie's Public Speaking for Success (Tarcher) and How to Win Friends & Influence People (Pocket)

"A lively introduction to the world of speaking professionally, and while it's fun to read, it provides solid and important information. I highly recommend it."

—Bill Gurstelle, producer of the PBS television show MAKE:Television

"Scott writes with both wit and wisdom. [He] had me laughing one moment, then in the next scurrying off to fix one of my upcoming talks.... This book did more to relieve my fears and raise the level of my speaking than any book I've read."

—Bill Scott, director of UI engineering at Netflix;
coauthor of O'Reilly's Designing Web Interfaces

"Berkun takes you down the path of the experienced speaker. It's not about slides, it's not even about your words, it's about a performance that marries the two together and lets people walk away with at least one new idea."

—Brady Forrest, O'Reilly Radar/Ignite! co-creator

"If you have to give just one speech in your life, Chapter 5 is worth the cover price alone. *Confessions of a Public Speaker* lays out the traps that can turn a good idea into a bad speech, all wrapped in Berkun's entertaining style of layering myth and science with clear writing."

—Matt Waite, principal developer at Politifact.com;
2009 Pulitzer Prize winner

"This is a helpful, funny, useful, and most of all *truthful* book about public speaking. Read this, and you'll never give (or listen to) a talk the same way again."

—Erin McKean, TED 2007 speaker; CEO of Wordnik

"The definitive guidebook for every speaker. Berkun's masterpiece shows how speakers really feel, what they really do, and what it takes to turn your foibles and fears into great speeches, time after time. The most useful, fun book I've ever read on anything."

—Robert Sutton, professor, Stanford University;
author of The No Asshole Rule (Business Plus)

"Scott Berkun has written the book I wish I had read before I started speaking publicly. He's described every bad experience I ever had and what I learned, painstakingly, to do about it.... And to top it all off, it's a really entertaining read!"

—Jared Spool, User Interface Engineering

"Great war stories from the field. Great real-life stories. I felt I was there.... And these lessons were learned the hard way."

*—Richard Klees, president of Communication Power (presentation coach for the Fortune 500)*

"Scott Berkun offers an approachable and practical guide for taking apart and understanding the art of presentations. Berkun's extensive experiences shine a bright light of understanding on the core fear regarding public speaking—much of what terrifies you exists entirely in your mind."

*—Michael Lopp, author of* Managing Humans *(Apress)*

"Although perhaps urban legend, I have read in different sources that public speaking on many people's lists beats out death as a phobia... without any doubt, any speech-phobe who reads Scott Berkun's book will lose the anxiety they possess and in turn will leave the audience spellbound."

*—Richard Saul Wurman, founder and creator of the TED Conference*

# confessions of a
# public speaker

# confessions of a
# public speaker

scott berkun

O'REILLY®

Beijing • Cambridge • Farnham • Köln • Sebastopol • Taipei • Tokyo

# Confessions of a Public Speaker

by Scott Berkun

Published by O'Reilly Media, Inc., 1005 Gravenstein Highway North, Sebastopol, CA 95472.

O'Reilly books may be purchased for educational, business, or sales promotional use. Online editions are also available for most titles (*http://my.safaribooksonline.com*). For more information, contact our corporate/institutional sales department: (800) 998-9938 or *corporate@oreilly.com*.

**Editor:** Mary Treseler
**Production Editor:**
 Rachel Monaghan
**Copyeditor:** Marlowe Shaeffer
**Proofreader:** Rachel Monaghan

**Indexer:** Angela Howard
**Interior Designer:** Ron Bilodeau
**Cover Designer:**
 Monica Kamsvaag
**Illustrator:** Robert Romano

**Printing History:**

October 2009:  First Edition.

 This book uses RepKover™, a durable and lay-flat binding.

ISBN: 978-0-596-80199-1
[C]                                                                [12/09]

# Contents

# Disclaimer

This book is highly opinionated, personal, and full of behind-the-scenes stories. You may not like this. Some people like seeing how sausage is made, but many do not.

Although everything in this book is true and written to be useful, if you don't always want to hear the truth, this book might not be for you.

This book is written with faith in the idea that if we all spoke thoughtfully and listened carefully, the world would be a better place.

## CHAPTER 1

# I can't see you naked

I'm on a long flight from Seattle to Belgium, and the woman sitting next to me starts a conversation. Despite hiding behind the book in my hands, I'm now forced into a common and sometimes unfortunate air-travel situation: the gamble of talking to a stranger I can't escape from. While it's fun to be near someone interesting for occasional chats, being stuck next to a person who will not stop talking for nine hours is my idea of hell. (And you never know which it will be until after you start talking, when it's too late.) Not wanting to be rude, I say hello. She asks what I do for a living, at which I pause. I've been down this bumpy conversational road many times. You see, I have two answers, and both suck.

The best answer I have is I'm a writer. I write books and essays. But saying I'm a writer is bad because people get excited I might be Dan Brown, John Grisham, or Dave Eggers, someone famous they can tell their friends they met. When they learn I'm one of the millions of writers they've never heard of—and not someone whose novel was turned into a blockbuster movie—they fall into a kind of disappointment never experienced by people who are employed as lawyers, plumbers, or even assistant fry cooks at McDonald's.

My other choice is worse, which is to say I'm a public speaker. If you tell people you're a public speaker, they'll assume one of three bad things:

1. You're a motivational speaker who wears bad suits, sweats too much, and dreams about Tony Robbins.

2. You're a high priest in a cult and will soon try to convert them to your religion.

3. You're single, unemployed, and live in a van down by the river.

I don't want to call myself a public speaker. Professors, executives, pundits, and politicians all spend much of their professional lives speaking in public, but they don't call themselves public speakers either. And for good reason. Public speaking is a form of expression. You have to do it about a topic, and whatever that topic is defines you better than the actual speaking does. But I speak about the things I write about, which can be just about anything. Calling myself a freelance thinker—as vacuous as it sounds—is accurate, but if I say it, someone would surely think I'm unemployed, just as I would if a stranger on an airplane said it to me. Yet freelance thinking is why I'm on the plane. I quit my regular job years ago, wrote two bestselling books, and have been hired to fly to Brussels to speak about ideas from those books.

I explain all this to my newfound flight friend. Her first question, one I often hear at this point in conversations, is: "When you're giving a lecture, do you imagine everyone in the room naked?" She's half-joking but also eyeing me strangely. She wants an answer. I want to say of course I don't. No one does. You're never told to imagine people naked at your job interview or at the dentist, and for good reason. Being naked or imagining naked people in the daytime makes most things more complicated, not less, which is one of the reasons we invented clothes. Despite it being very bad advice, it's somehow the one universally known tip for public speaking.

I asked many experts, and not one knew who first offered this advice, though the best guess is Winston Churchill,[1] who may have claimed imagining the audience naked worked for him. But he was also known for drinking a bottle of champagne and a fifth of brandy or more a day. With that much alcohol, you might need to imagine people naked just to stay awake. For us mere mortals (Churchill had an amazing tolerance for alcohol), you won't find a single public-speaking expert recommending thoughts of naked people, nor a fifth of brandy. Yet, if you tell a friend you're nervous about a presentation you have to give at work tomorrow, naked people will be mentioned within 30 seconds. I can't explain why. It seems bad advice that's fun will always be better known than good advice that's dull—no matter how useless that fun advice is.

In hundreds of lectures around the world, I've done most of the scary, tragic, embarrassing things that terrify people. I've been heckled by drunken crowds in a Boston bar. I've lectured to empty seats, and a bored janitor, in New York City. I've had a laptop crash in a Moscow auditorium; a microphone die at a keynote

---

1 I asked more than a dozen experts, and while none knew of the origins of the advice, Richard I. Garber tracked down a mention in expert James C. Humes's book *The Sir Winston Method* (Quill) connecting Churchill to it.

speech in San Jose; and I've watched helplessly as the Parisian executives who hired me fell asleep in the conference room while I was speaking. The secret to coping with these events is to realize everyone forgets about them after they happen—except for one person: me. No one else really cares that much.

When I'm up there speaking, I remind myself of the last time I was in row 25 of the auditorium, or in the corner of a boardroom, or back in some stupid class in high school, desperately trying not to daydream or fall asleep. Most people listening to presentations around the world right now are hoping their speakers will end soon. That's all they want. They're not judging as much as you think, because they don't care as much as you think. Knowing this helps enormously. If some disaster happens, something explodes or I trip and fall, I'll have more attention from the audience than I probably had 30 seconds before. And if I don't care that much about my disaster, I can use the attention I've earned and do something good with it—whatever I say next, they are sure to remember. And if nothing else, my tragedy will give everyone in the audience a funny story to share. The laughter from that story will do more good for the world than anything my presentation, or any other that day, probably would have done anyway.

And so, if during my next lecture in Philadelphia, my shoes burst into flames or I fall down some steps and land face-first in the aisle, I can turn what's happening into an opportunity. I'm now cast in a story that will be told more often than anything mentioned in any other speech that month. The story will get better and more scandalous as it's told, eventually including something about drunk, naked people. Best of all, I earn the right to tell that story in the future when a lesser disaster occurs. I can choose to use one supposed catastrophe as an escape from the next: "You think this is embarrassing? Well, back in Philly...." And on it goes.

If you'd like to be good at something, the first thing to go out the window is the notion of perfection. Every time I get up to the front of the room, I know I will make mistakes. And this is OK. If you examine how we talk to one another every day, including people giving presentations, you'll find that even the best speakers make tons of mistakes. Michael Erard, author of *Um* (Anchor), a study of how we talk, offers this:

*They [mistakes] occur on average once every ten words.... If people say an average of 15,000 words each day, that's about 1,500 verbal blunders a day. Next time you say something, listen to yourself carefully. You st-st-stutter; you forget the words, you swotch the sounds (and when you type, you reverse the lttres—and prhps omt thm too). The bulk of these go unnoticed or brushed aside, but they're all fascinating, as much as for why they're ignored as why they're noticed.*

If you listen to Martin Luther King, Malcolm X, or Winston Churchill, and then read the unedited transcripts of those same speeches, you'll find mistakes. However, they're mistakes we commonly ignore because we're incredibly forgiving of spoken language.[2] Sentences get abandoned mid-thought and phrases are repeated, but we correct these errors in our minds all the time, even for people who are supposed to be fantastic speakers. As long as the message comes through, people naturally overlook many things. Lincoln had a high-pitched voice. Dale Carnegie had a Southern twang. Cicero used to hyperventilate. Barbara Walters, Charles Darwin, Winston Churchill, and even Moses had stutters, lisps, or other speech issues, but that didn't end their careers, because they had interesting messages to share with people. As superficial as public speaking can seem, history bears out that people with clear ideas and strong points are the ones we remember.

I know I make small mistakes all the time. There's no way not to. Besides, when performing, perfection is boring. Tyler Durden, the quasi-hero from the film *Fight Club*, said to stop being perfect because obsessing about perfection stops you from growing. You stop taking chances, which means you stop learning. I don't want to be perfect. I want be useful, I want to be good, and I want to sound like myself. Trying to be perfect gets in the way of all three. If anything, making some mistakes or stumbling in a couple of places reminds everyone of how hard it is to stand up at the front of the room in the first place. Mistakes will happen—what matters more is how you frame your mistakes, and there are two ways to do this:

---

2 Some speeches are more formal than others, so you *can* find examples of perfect readings (but these are uncommon). I listened to *Greatest Speeches of All Time*, Vol. I and Vol. II, and many speeches support this point.

1. Avoid the mistake of trying to make no mistakes. You should work hard to know your material, but also know you won't be perfect. This way, you won't be devastated when small things go wrong.

2. Know that your response to a mistake defines the audience's response. If I respond to spilling water on my pants as if it were the sinking of the *Titanic*, the audience will see it, and me, as a tragedy. But if I'm cool, or better yet, find it funny, the audience will do the same.

As an illustrative mistake of my own, in March 2008 I gave a keynote talk about creativity to a crowd of 2,000 people at the Web 2.0 Expo conference. I was given 10 minutes to speak, and since the average person speaks 2–3 words per second, all you need is 1,500 words of material (600 seconds × 2.5 words per second). Ten minutes seems tough, but many great speeches in history were much shorter, including Lincoln's Gettysburg Address and Jesus' Sermon on the Mount. It's plenty of time if I know what I want to say. I prepared my talk, practiced it well, and showed up early to get a walkthrough before the crowd arrived. The tech crew showed me the stage, the lectern, and the remote for controlling my slides. Below the stage was a countdown timer that would show my remaining time. Nice.

The tech crew was adamant about one fact: the remote control only had a forward button. If I wanted to go back to a previous slide, I had to ask them, over the microphone, to go backward. I'd never seen this before. All remotes let you navigate forward and backward—why would someone go out of his way to eliminate the back button? I never got an answer.[3] But since my talk was so short, and I rarely needed to go backward anyway, I didn't worry. I made a mental note to avoid accidentally hitting the button on the kamikaze remote. Piece of cake, I thought.

Standing backstage, listening to the last speaker before my turn, Edwin Aoki from AOL, I saw the huge crowd in the darkness. Press photographers and film crews knelt down in the aisles, the glare of the lights reflecting in their lenses making them easy to find.

---

[3] For keynotes at some large events, there are several computers set up to run the same slides just in case one crashes. For it to work, the remote control is attached to the custom system, not to any one computer; thus, the funky remote.

Aoki finished to applause, and Brady Forrest, the co-host of the event, stepped out on the stage to introduce me. I was psyched and ready. I'd practiced. I knew my material. I had big ideas and fun stories. I was confident it would be great. I heard my name and charged the stage, heading straight for the lectern. My eyes were fixed on the remote control, the one thing I needed before I could start. I carefully placed my fingers on the side of the remote to ensure I didn't hit the button by accident (as you can see in Figure 1-1). Finally, I was ready to go.

*Figure 1-1. Live at Web 2.0 Expo. You can see the kamikaze remote control in my left hand.*

My brain snapped into gear and I looked out into the crowd to get my bearings. My eyes, on their way back to the center of the room, stopped at the countdown timer. There I found a surprise. Instead of the 10 minutes I expected—the 10 minutes I'd planned, prepared, and practiced for—I had only 9 minutes and 34 seconds. Twenty-six of my precious seconds were gone.

I confess here in the comforts of this book, with no audience and no pressure, 26 seconds doesn't seem worth complaining about.

It's barely enough time to tie your shoelaces. But there in the moment, raring to go, I was caught off guard. I couldn't imagine how I wasted 26 seconds without starting. (I'd learn later that Brady's introduction and my walk across the big stage explained the lapse.) And as I tried to make sense of this surprising number, more time went by. My brain—not as smart as it thinks it is—insisted on playing detective right there, live on stage, consuming even more precious time. I don't know why my brain did this, but my brain does many curious things I have to figure out later.

Meanwhile, I'm rambling. Blah blah innovation blah creativity blah. I'm not a blabbermouth in real life, but for 15 seconds I can ramble on about a subject I know well enough to seem like I'm *not* rambling. Doing this bought me just enough time for my brain to give up its pointless investigation of what happened. Finally focused, I had to waste even more time managing the surgery-like segue between my rambles and the first point of my prepared material. Confidently back on track, despite being a full minute behind, I hit the remote to advance the slide. But when I did, I held it too long and two slides flew by.

We all have reserve tanks of strength that help us cope when things go wrong, but here mine hit empty. I didn't have the courage to stop my talk, ask the tech folks over the microphone—as if speaking to the gods above—to go back, while just standing there on stage, waiting helplessly as the clock ate even more of my precious seconds. So, I pressed on, did my best, and fled the stage after my 10 minutes ended.

It was a disaster to me. I never found my rhythm and couldn't remember much of what I'd said. But as I talked with people I knew in the audience, I discovered something much more interesting. Not only did no one care, no one noticed. The drama was mostly in my own mind. As Dale Carnegie wrote in *Public Speaking for Success:*[4]

> Good speakers usually find when they finish that there have been four versions of the speech: the one they delivered, the one they prepared, the one the newspapers say was delivered, and the one on the way home they wish they had delivered.

---

[4] (Tarcher), p. 61.

You can watch the 10-minute video of the talk and see for yourself.[5] It's not an amazing presentation, but it's not a bad one either. Whatever mistakes and imperfections exist, they're larger in my head than in yours. My struggles on stage that night taught me a lesson: never plan to use the full time given. Had I planned to go 9 minutes instead of 10, I wouldn't have cared what the clock said, how weird the remote was, or how long it took me to cross the stage.

And it's often the case that the things speakers obsess about are the opposite of what the audience cares about. They want to be entertained. They want to learn. And most of all, they want you to do well. Many mistakes you can make while performing do not prevent those things from happening. It's the mistakes you make before you even say a word that matter more. These include the mistakes of not having an interesting opinion, of not thinking clearly about your points, and of not planning ways to make those points relevant to your audience. Those are the ones that make the difference. If you can figure out how to get those right, not much else will matter.

---

5  Forty-eight seconds into the video, you can see the expression on my face as I see two of my slides fly by: *http://www.blip.tv/file/856263/*.

## CHAPTER 2

# The attack of the butterflies

*"The best speakers know enough to be scared...the only difference between the pros and the novices is that the pros have trained the butterflies to fly in formation."*
—Edward R. Murrow

While there are good reasons why people fear public speaking, until I see someone flee from the lectern mid-presentation, running for his life through the fire exit on stage left, we can't say public speaking is scarier than death. This oddly popular factoid, commonly stated as, "Did you know people would rather die than speak in public?", is a classic case of why you should ask people how they know what they think they know. This "fact" implies that people will, if given the chance, choose to jump off buildings or swallow cyanide capsules rather than give a short presentation to their coworkers. Since this doesn't happen in the real world—no suicide note has ever mentioned an upcoming presentation as the reason for leaving this world—it's worth asking: where does this factoid come from?

The source is *The Book of Lists* by David Wallechinksy et al. (William Morrow), a trivia book first published in 1977. It included a list of things people are afraid of, and public speaking came in at number one. Here's the list, titled "The Worst Human Fears":

1. Speaking before a group
2. Heights
3. Insects and bugs
4. Financial problems
5. Deep water
6. Sickness
7. Death
8. Flying
9. Loneliness
10. Dogs
11. Driving/Riding in a car
12. Darkness
13. Elevators
14. Escalators

14

shot from behind his seat, which points out one major a
of giving a lecture: it's unlikely someone will sne
behind you to do you in without the audience no
stage behind a lectern gave safety to President C
his last public appearance in Iraq when
reporter threw one, then a second, sh
onslaught from the stage, Bush had
dodged them both.

The real danger is always in t
The Who, Pearl Jam, and
the stands. And althoug
ously explode whil
have ever been re
crowds is wh
escape, wh
stage,
sho

When thinking about fun things like death, bad surveys, and public speaking, the best place to start is with the realization that no has died from giving a bad presentation. Well, at least one person did, President William Henry Harrison, but he developed pneumonia after giving the longest inaugural address in U.S. history. The easy lesson from his story: keep it short, or you might die. This exception aside, by the time you're important enough— like Gandhi or Lincoln—for someone to want to kill you, it's not the public speaking that's going to do you in. Malcolm X was shot at the beginning of a speech in 1965, but he was a fantastic speaker (if anything, he was killed because he spoke too well). Lincoln was assassinated *watching* other people on stage. He was

---

1 *The Book of Lists* doesn't say, but it's likely that its source was the 1973 report published by the Bruskin/Goldkin agency.

2 If you combined this list to create the scariest thing possible, it would be to give a presentation in an airplane at 35,000 feet, near a spider web, while doing your taxes, sitting in the deep end of a pool inside the airplane, feeling ill, with the lights out, next to a rabid dog, near an escalator that leads to an elevator.

dvantage
ak up from
cing. Being on
George W. Bush in
in disgust, an Iraqi
e at him. Watching the
the advantage and nimbly

he crowds. Fans of rock bands like
the Rolling Stones have been killed in
the drummer for Spinal Tap did mysteri-
performing, very few real on-stage deaths
orted in the history of the world. The danger of
some people prefer the aisle seats—they can quickly
ether they're fleeing from fire or boredom. If you're on
ot only do you have better access to the fire exits, but
d you faint, fall down, or suffer a heart attack, everyone in
tendance will know immediately and call an ambulance for you.
The next time you're at the front of the room to give a presentation, you should know that, by all logic, you are the safest person
there. The problem is that our brains are wired to believe the
opposite; see Figure 2-1.

*Figure 2-1. When you see the left, your brain sees the right.*

Our brains, for all their wonders, identify the following four
things as being very bad for survival:

- Standing alone
- In open territory with no place to hide

- Without a weapon
- In front of a large crowd of creatures staring at you

In the long history of all living things, any situation where all the above were true was very bad for you. It meant the odds were high that you would soon be attacked and eaten alive. Many predators hunt in packs, and their easiest prey are those who stand alone, without a weapon, on a flat area of land where there is little cover (e.g., a stage). Our ancestors, the ones who survived, developed a fear response to these situations. So, despite my 15 years of teaching classes, running workshops, and giving lectures, no matter how comfortable I appear to the audience when at the front of the room, it's a scientific fact that my brain and body will experience some kind of fear before and often while I'm speaking.

The design of the brain's wiring—given its long operational history, which is hundreds of thousands of years older than the history of public speaking, or speaking at all, for that matter—makes it impossible to stop fearing what it knows is the worst tactical situation for a person to be in. There is no way to turn it off, at least not completely. This wiring is so primal that it lives in the oldest part of our brains where, like many of the brain's other important functions, we have almost no control.

Take, for example, the simple act of breathing. Right now, try to hold your breath. The average person can go for a minute or so, but as the pain intensifies—pain generated by your nervous system to stop you from doing stupid things like killing yourself—your body will eventually force you to give in. Your brain desperately wants you to live and will do many things without asking permission to help you survive. Even if you're particularly stubborn and you make yourself pass out from lack of oxygen, guess what happens? You live anyway. Your ever-faithful amygdala, one of the oldest parts of your brain, takes over, continuing to regulate your breathing, heart rate, and a thousand other things you never think about until you come to your senses (literally and figuratively).

For years, I was in denial about my public speaking fears. After seeing me speak, when people asked whether I get nervous, I always did the stupid machismo thing. I'd smirk, as if to say, "Who me? Only mere mortals get nervous." At some level, I'd always known my answer was bullshit, but I didn't know the science, nor had I studied what others had to say. It turns out there are consistent reports from famous public figures confirming that, despite their talents and success, their brains have the same wiring as ours:

- Mark Twain, who made most of his income from speaking, not writing, said, "There are two types of speakers: those that are nervous and those that are liars."

- Elvis Presley said, "I've never gotten over what they call stage fright. I go through it every show."

- Thomas Jefferson was so afraid of public speaking that he had someone else read the State of the Union address (George Washington didn't like speaking either).[3]

- Bono, of U2, claims to get nervous the morning of every one of the thousands of shows he's performed.

- Winston Churchill, John F. Kennedy, Margaret Thatcher, Barbara Walters, Johnny Carson, Barbra Streisand, and Ian Holm have all reported fears of public communication.[4]

- Aristotle, Isaac Newton, Charles Darwin, Winston Churchill, John Updike, Jack Welch, and James Earl Jones all had stutters and were nervous speakers at one time in their lives.[5]

Even if you could completely shut off these fear-response systems, which is the first thing people with fears of public speaking want to do, it would be a bad idea for two reasons. First, having the old parts of our brains in control of our fear responses is a good thing. If a legion of escaped half-lion, half-ninja warriors were to fall through the ceiling and surround you—with the sole mission of converting your fine flesh into thin sandwich-ready slices—do you want the burden of consciously deciding how fast to increase your heart rate, or which muscles to fire first to get your legs moving so you can run away? Your conscious mind cannot work fast enough to do these things in the small amount of time you'd have to survive. It's good that fear responses are controlled by the subconscious

---

3  It is debated what the motivations were for Jefferson's small number of speeches. The Jefferson Library takes a decidedly generous view: see *http://wiki.monticello. org/mediawiki/index.php/Public_Speaking* and Halford Ryan's *U.S. Presidents As Orators: A Bio-Critical Sourcebook* (Greenwood Press).

4  From *Conquer Your Speech Anxiety*, Karen Kangas Dwyer (Wadsworth).

5  *The Francis Effect*, M. F. Fensholt (Oakmont Press), p. 286.

parts of our minds, since those are the only parts with fast enough wires to do anything useful when real danger happens.

The downside is that this fear-response wiring causes problems because our lives today are very safe. Few of us are regularly chased by lions or wrestle alligators on our way to work, making our fear-response programming out of sync with much of modern life. As a result, the same stress responses we used for survival for millions of years get applied to nonsurvival situations by our eager brains. We develop ulcers, high blood pressure, headaches, and other physical problems in part because our stress systems aren't designed to handle the "dangers" of our brave new world: computer crashes, micromanaging bosses, 12-way conference calls, and long commutes in rush-hour traffic. If we were chased by tigers on the way to give a presentation, we'd likely find the presentation not nearly as scary—our perspective on what things are worth fearing would have been freshly calibrated.

Second, fear focuses attention. All the fun, interesting things in life come with fears. Want to ask that cute girl out on a date? Thinking of applying for that cool job? Want to write a novel? Start a company? All good things come with the possibility of failure, whether it's rejection, disappointment, or embarrassment, and fear of those failures is what motivates many people to do the work necessary to be successful. That fear gives us the energy to proactively prevent failures from happening. Many psychological causes of fear in work situations—being laughed at by coworkers or looking stupid in front of the boss—can also be seen as opportunities to impress or prove your value. Curiously enough, there may be little difference biologically between fear of failure and anticipation of success. In his excellent book *Brain Rules* (Pear Press), Dr. John Medina points out that it is very difficult for the body to distinguish between states of arousal and states of anxiety:

> *Many of the same mechanisms that cause you to shrink in horror from a predator are also used when you are having sex— or even while you are consuming your Thanksgiving dinner. To your body, saber-toothed tigers and orgasms and turkey gravy look remarkably similar. An aroused physiological state is characteristic of both stress and pleasure.*

Assuming he's right, why would this be? In both cases, it's because your body has prepared energy for you to use. The body doesn't care whether it's for good reasons or bad, it just knows it must prepare for something to happen. If you pretend to have no fears of public speaking, you deny yourself the natural energy your body is giving you. Anxiety creates a kind of energy you can use, just as excitement does. Ian Tyson, a stand-up comedian and motivational speaker, offered this gem of advice: "The body's reaction to fear and excitement is the same...so it becomes a mental decision: am I afraid or am I excited?" If the body can't tell the difference, it's up to you to use your instincts to help rather than hurt you. The best way to do this is to plan before you speak. When you are actually giving a presentation, there are many variables out of your control—it's OK and normal to have some fear of them. But in the days or hours beforehand, you can do many things to prepare yourself and take control of the factors you *can* do something about.

## What to do before you speak

The main advantage a speaker has over the audience is knowing what comes next. Comedians—the best public speakers—achieve what they do largely because you don't see the punch lines coming. To create a similar advantage, I, like George Carlin or Chris Rock, practice my material. It's the only way I learn how to get from one point to another, or to tell each story or fact in the best way to set up the next one. And when I say I practice, I mean I stand up at my desk, imagine an audience around me, and present exactly as if it were the real thing. If I plan to do something in the presentation, I practice it. But I don't practice to make perfect, and I don't memorize. If I did either, I'd sound like a robot, or worse, like a person trying very hard to say things in an exact, specific, and entirely unnatural style, which people can spot a mile away. My intent is simply to know my material so well that I'm very comfortable with it. Confidence, not perfection, is the goal.

Can you guess what most people who are worried about their presentations refuse to do? Practice. When I'm asked to coach someone on his presentation, and he sends me his slides, do you know the first question I ask? "Did you practice?" Usually he says no, surprised this would be so important. As if other performers like rock bands and Shakespearean actors don't need to rehearse to get their material right. The slides are not the performance: you, the speaker, are the performance. And it turns out, most of the advice you find in all the great books on public speaking, including advice about slides, is difficult to apply if you don't practice. The most pragmatic reason for practice is that it allows me to safely make mistakes and correct them before anyone ever sees it. It's possible I'm not a better public speaker than anyone else—I'm just better at catching and fixing problems.

When I practice, especially with a draft of new material, I run into many issues. And when I stumble or get confused, I stop and make a choice:

- Can I make this work if I try it again?
- Does this slide or the previous one need to change?
- Can a photograph and a story replace all this text?
- Is there a better lead-in to this point from the previous point?
- Will things improve if I just rip this point/slide/idea out completely?

I repeat this process until I can get through the entire talk without making major mistakes. Since I'm more afraid of giving a horrible presentation than I am of practicing for a few hours, practice wins. The energy from my fear of failing and looking stupid in front of a crowd fuels me to work harder to prevent that from happening. It's that simple.

Now, while everyone is free to practice—it requires no special intelligence or magic powers—most people don't because:

- It's not fun
- It takes time
- They feel silly doing it
- They assume no one else does
- Their fear of speaking leads to procrastination, creating a self-fulfilling prophecy of misery

I know I look like an idiot practicing a presentation in my underwear at home, talking to a room of imaginary people. When I practice in hotel rooms, which I often do, I'm worried that at any moment the maid will barge in mid-sentence, and I'll have to attempt to explain why on earth I'm lecturing to myself in my underwear. But I'd rather face those fears in the comfort of my own room—with my own mini-bar, on my own time, over and over as many times as I wish—than in front of a real crowd, a crowd that is likely capturing my performance on videos and podcasts, recording what I'm doing for all time. There are no do-overs when you're doing the real thing.

By the time I present to an actual audience, it's not really the first time at all. In fact, by the third or fourth time I practice a talk, I can do a decent job without any slides, as I've learned how to make the key points by heart. The confidence that comes from practicing makes it possible to improvise and respond to unexpected things—like hecklers, tough questions, bored audiences, or equipment failures—that might occur during the talk. If I hadn't practiced, I'd be so worried about my material that I'd be unable to pay attention to anything else, much less anticipate what's coming from the audience. I admit that even with all my practice I may still do a bad job, make mistakes, or disappoint the crowd, but I can be certain the cause will not be that I was afraid of, or confused by, my own slides. An entire universe of fears and mistakes goes away simply by having confidence in your material.

But even with all the practice in the world, my body, like yours, will still decide for itself when to be afraid. Consider, for example, the strange world of sweaty palms. Why would sweaty palms be of use in life-or-death situations? I've had sweaty palms only once, right before I was televised on CNBC. At the start of the taping, sitting on an uncomfortable pink couch, trying to stay calm in the bright lights and cold air, I felt a strange lightness in my palms. With the cameras rolling, I held up my hands to see what was going on. I had to touch them to realize they were sweating. The weirdo that I am, I found this really funny, which, by coincidence, relieved some of my anxiety. The best theory from scientists is that primates, creatures who climb things, have greater dexterity if their hands are damp. It's the same reason why you touch your thumb to your tongue before turning a page of a newspaper. My point is that parts of your body will respond in ancient ways to stress, no matter how prepared you are.[6] That's OK.

---

[6] The attack of stomach butterflies is still a mystery. The best guess is that it's a side effect of your stress response, moving blood away from your digestive system to more important parts of your body for survival. Peeing and related excrementous activity in your pants has similar motivations, plus the bonus effect of distracting whatever is trying to eat you away from your tasty flesh.

It doesn't mean you're weird or a coward, it just means your body is trying hard to save your life. It's nice of your body to do this in the same way it's nice of your dog to protect you from squirrels. It's hard to blame a dog for its instinctive behavior, and the same understanding should be applied to your own brain.

Since I respect my body's unstoppable fear responses, I have to go out of my way to calm down before I give a presentation. I want to make my body as relaxed as possible and exhaust as much physical energy early in the day. As a rule, I go to the gym the morning before a talk, with the goal of releasing any extra nervous energy before I get on stage. It's the only way I've found to naturally turn down those fear responses and lower the odds they'll fire. Other ways to reduce physical stress include:

- Getting to the venue early so you don't have to rush
- Doing tech and sound rehearsal well before your start time
- Walking around the stage so your body feels safe in the room
- Sitting in the audience so you have a physical sense of what they will see
- Eating early enough so you won't be hungry, but not right before your talk
- Talking to some people in the audience before you start (if it suits you), so it's no longer made up of strangers (friends are less likely to try to eat you)

All of these things allow you to get used to the physical environment you will be speaking in, which should minimize your body's sense of danger. A sound check lets your ears hear how you will sound when speaking, just as a stroll across the stage helps your body feel like it knows the terrain. These might seem like small things, but you must control all the factors you can to compensate for the bigger ones, the ones that arise during your talking that you can't control. Speakers who arrive late, change their slides at the last minute, or never walk the stage until it's their turn to speak, and then complain about anxiety, have only themselves to blame. It's not the actual speaking that's the problem; they're failing to take responsibility for their body's unchangeable responses to stress.

There are also psychological reasons why public speaking is scary. These include fears like:

- Being judged, criticized, or laughed at
- Doing something embarrassing in front of other people
- Saying something stupid the crowd will never forget
- Boring people to sleep even when you say your best idea

We can minimize most of these fears by realizing that we speak in public all the time. You're already good at public speaking—the average person says 15,000 words a day.[7] Unless you are reading this locked in solitary confinement, most of the words you say are said to other people. If you have a social life and go out on Friday night, you probably speak to two, three, or even five people all at the same time. Congratulations, you are already a practiced, successful public speaker. You speak to your coworkers, your family, and your friends. You use email and the Web, so you write things that are seen by hundreds of people every day. If you look back at the list of fears, they all apply in these situations as well.

In fact, there is a greater likelihood of being judged by people you know because they care about what you say. They have reasons to argue and disagree since what you do will affect them in ways a public speaker never can. An audience of strangers cares little and, at worst, will daydream or fall asleep, rendering them incapable of noticing any mistakes you make. While it's true that many fears are irrational and can't be dispelled by mere logic, if you can talk comfortably to people you know, then you possess the skills needed to speak to groups of people you don't know. Pay close attention the next time you're listening to a good public speaker. The speaker is probably natural and comfortable, making you feel as though he's talking to a small group, despite how many people are actually in the audience.

Having a sense of control, even if it's just in your mind, is important for many performers. If you watch athletes and musicians, people who perform in front of massive crowds nightly, they all have preshow rituals. LeBron James and Mike Bibby, all-star basketball players, chew their nails superstitiously before and during games. Michael Jordan wore his old University of North Carolina shorts under his NBA shorts in every game. Wayne Gretzky

---

[7]  There is a wide range from 10,000–20,000, depending on the individual. (This data comes from Michael Erard's *Um* [Anchor].) I wish you could know the number for the person sitting next to you on a plane before you start talking to him.

tucked his jersey into his hockey pants, something he learned to do before games as a kid. Wade Boggs ate chicken before every single game. These small acts of control, however random or bizarre they seem to us, helped give them the confidence needed to face the out-of-control reality of their jobs. And their jobs are much harder than what public speakers do. For every point Michael Jordan ever scored, there was another well-paid professional athlete, or team of athletes, trying very hard to stop him from doing so.

So, unless presentation terrorists steal your microphone mid-sentence or put up their own projector and start showing their own slide deck—designed specifically to contradict your every point—you're free from the pressures other performers face nightly. Small observations like this make it easier to laugh at nerves, even if they won't go away.

## CHAPTER 3

# $30,000 an hour

It's 7:47 a.m. at Fisherman's Wharf in San Francisco, so early the sun is just starting to rise. It's an ungodly time and place for any writer to be outside. Writers aren't the most well-adjusted people, and it's telling that our preferred means of interaction with civilization is throwing paragraph-shaped grenades at people from behind the safety of a laptop. I know few writers who love mornings, and the doorman at my hotel—who wears a bright blue sailor's uniform as part of the nautical-themed thrill ride that is the Argonaut Hotel—is clearly on my side. He waves down a cab for me and gives a half-smile from underneath his tired eyes, a smile that says, "Doesn't it suck to work this early?" Anyone who finishes the night shift with a sense of humor is a good man indeed. Or perhaps I just look like trash this morning and he finds my appearance entertaining. Maybe it's both.

People talk about sunrises as if they were magical things. Yet here at Fisherman's Wharf, the morning fog forming a glorious orange blanket around a late-winter sunrise, no one except the doorman, the cab driver, and me is awake and outside. You know why? People are lazy. Even if there was a sunrise at 7:47 a.m. as brilliant and soul-stirring as a wall-sized J. M. W. Turner masterpiece, a sunrise giving out $100 bills and tomorrow's lottery numbers, few of us would be out to see it. Most of the things we say are so wonderful and amazing will lose without a fight to an extra hour of sleep. We'd wake up, think it over for a few moments, and fall back into the comfort of our dreams. Sleep deprivation is a curse of the modern age, a problem born from our technological things. Before Edison's light bulb, we averaged 10 hours a night; in 2009, we average nearly half that.[1] And this means, when it comes to sunrises, judge people by what they do, not what they say.

On this morning, the sun is putting on quite a show, but where are all the sunrise-lovers? They're not with me out on the street. They're sleeping, just as I would be if I could. The truth is, public speakers everywhere would have an easier time keeping their audiences awake if more people actually slept well the night before. If the ascension of our nearest star—the source of all energy and

---

[1] There is good anecdotal evidence suggesting that, before electricity, most Americans had natural patterns of sleeping soon after sunset and rising at sunrise. There's harder data about recent trends: *http://www.usatoday.com/news/health/ 2007-08-29-sleep-study_N.htm.*

life on earth, the universal symbol for all that is good, happy, and hopeful—can't get people out of bed, what chance does a speaker have?

In all honesty, I love the sunrise…it's the getting up to see it I hate. Sunrises are transcendent when viewed through a hotel window, from a comfy bed, when I'm not expected to do anything for anyone for hours. My professional problem is that public speaking is often scheduled hundreds of minutes on the wrong side of noon. And on the days I'm lucky enough to get top billing for an event, I earn an additional chronological treat: the keynote means I'm to set the tone for the day, a challenge that—given our limited understanding of space and time—requires me to speak before anyone else. All this explains why, at 7:48 a.m. on a Tuesday, I am showered, cleaned, shaved, pruned, fed, and deodorized, wearing a pressed shirt and shiny shoes, in a cab on my way to the San Francisco waterfront. Like the gorgeous light from the sun still conquering the clouds over the San Francisco Bay outside my cab window, this morning is both great and horrible, a thrill and a bore. It's an amazing way to live, getting paid to think and learn and exchange ideas—all things I love. But I'm far from home, going to an unfamiliar place, and performing for strangers, three stressful facts that mean anything can happen, especially since it's the worst of all times for my particular brain—early morning.

Making it to the venue is the first challenge a speaker-for-hire faces, and let me tell you, it's often a bigger challenge than the lecture itself. The lecture I know well, since I created it. I have no one to blame if it stinks. And when I do finally arrive at the room I'm to speak in—even if it's the worst room in the world—I can try to adapt to whatever problems it has. But until I get to the room, until I make my way through the airports, highways, cities, conference centers, office complexes, and parking lots, I can't begin to get ready. Being in transit means, psychologically speaking, you are in the purgatory of being *almost* there. Unlike lecturing, where I feel in control, it's the things I can't control that create stress— like the taxi driver getting lost, the traffic jam a handful of miles from where I'm supposed to be, and the confusing corporate and college campuses impossible for visitors like me to navigate. (How could anyone know Building 11 is next to Building 24 on Microsoft's main campus, or that the Kresge Auditorium is hiding behind Bexley Hall at MIT?) From experience, I know there is nothing worse than being in the strange territory of very close and surprisingly far at the same time.

When I arrive at the Fort Mason complex, the venue for this particular Tuesday, I discover, as my taxi roars off, that I'm far from where I need to be. Fort Mason is a sprawling Civil War–era military base, recently converted into a community center. The word *complex* is apt. My instructions say to find Building A, but there are no signs, and, more importantly, no normal-looking buildings, only endless rows of identical barracks, towers, and narrow parking lots (see Figure 3-1). The Fort Mason Center has one major flaw: it skipped the conversion. It still looks like a place designed to kill you, not welcome you to fun community activities. There are fences, gates, barricades, barbed wire, and tall stone walls with sharp corners.

***Figure 3-1.*** *The speaking venue: the intimidating Fort Mason, San Francisco.*

For comparison, there's a military museum in Kiev with two decommissioned World War II tanks at the main entrance, painted top to bottom with fun, peaceful swirls in bright rainbow colors (see Figure 3-2). Now that's a conversion: one day a death machine, the next a happy, silly plaything. Fort Mason, on the other hand, looks like a place the Spartans would say is too spartan.

They'd demand a row of shrubs and fresh paint before they'd even consider moving in.

*Figure 3-2. The National War Museum in Kiev, Ukraine. This is how to renovate a thing made for war.*

Trying to find my way, I stop at the front gate—which is what I do instinctively at gates near things looking like military bases—and only after long moments standing like an idiot do I realize I'm free to enter. No ID or white flag required. The gate is for cars, which explains the strange look from the guard: I'd been standing in the car lane the entire time. I wander aimlessly through the complex, surviving several dead ends, wrong turns, and unlabeled parking lots, trying not to imagine snipers in the towers above, until I find Building A and happily step inside.

The event at Fort Mason was run by Adaptive Path, a well-known Bay Area design consulting company, and I know these folks well. They've hired me before, and I say hello to friendly faces. I soon meet Julie, one of the event organizers, and after a brief chat she hands me an envelope. I know that inside is a check for $5,000, the fee for my services. I want to open it and look. My brain still thinks like a kid in terms of money, where $100 is tons and $500 is amazing. Anything over that simply does not exist in the surprisingly large 15-year-old part of my mind. I want to look inside, not because I don't trust Julie, but because I don't trust myself.

I'm baffled at how adults pay other adults so much for doing boring, safe, adult things. My childhood friend Doug drove his mom's Cadillac over the big hill on the wrong side of the entrance to the Whitestone Shopping Center in Queens at 60 miles per hour—with all of us screaming in the back seat—for free. He risked all of our lives without payment, other than his own insane but infectious pleasure. Meanwhile, bankers and hedge fund managers make millions playing with Excel spreadsheets, an activity with zero chance of bodily harm, save carpal tunnel syndrome. They earn more in a year than the guys who put the roof on my house, paved the road that leads to it, or work as firemen and policemen to protect it will see in a lifetime. It's curious facts like these we'll have to explain twice when the aliens land.

In the movies, gangsters are always opening briefcases and counting money, but in real life, no one does this. It's awkward, strange, and slimy. Money for Americans, a culture cursed by our unshakable Puritanical roots, is loaded with lust and shame. Yet, our modern consumer culture values the accumulation of financial wealth above all else, despite that little line of scripture about camels and needles suggesting that, for the faithful, this might be a bad idea.[2] The resulting contradiction causes much of what's wonderful and horrible about America. I suspect many of you jumped right to this chapter because of its title, or noticed it first when you skimmed through the table of contents. Not because you're evil, but because we're simultaneously fascinated and revolted by money, especially regarding work that seems superficial, like public speaking. I know I'm paid for something that, in the grand scheme, is not Work. It's work, with a little $w$, but it's not shoveling coal, building houses, or fighting in wars, which earn the capital $W$. I will never hurt my back, ruin my lungs, or get shot (unless I give a lecture at the next gang fight in the South Bronx). And despite the many questions that come to mind when Julie hands me that check, I cram it into my bag and head for the lectern where I can get to work.

I'm worth $5,000 a lecture and other speakers are worth $30,000 or more for two reasons: the lecture circuit and free

---

[2]  "…it is easier for a camel to go through the eye of a needle than for a rich man to enter the kingdom of God," Matthew 19:23–24. Or Timothy 6:10, "For the love of money is a root of all kinds of evil" (New International Version).

market economics.[3] People come up after I give a lecture and ask, "So when did you get on the lecture circuit?" And I respond by asking, "Do you know what the circuit is?" And they never have any idea. It's a term they've heard before, despite the fact that it's never explained, and it somehow seems to be the only reasonable thing to ask a public speaker when you're trying to seem interested in what he does for a living. Well, here's the primer. Public speaking, as a professional activity, became popular in the U.S. before the Civil War. In the 1800s—decades before electricity, radio, movies, television, the Internet, or automobiles—entertainment was hard to find. It explains why so many people sang in church choirs, read books, or actually *talked* to one another for hours on end: there was no competition.

In the 1820s, a man named Josiah Holbrook developed the idea of a lecture series called Lyceum, named after the Greek theater where Aristotle lectured his students (for free). It was amazingly popular, the *American Idol* of its day. People everywhere wanted it to come to their town. By 1835, there were 3,000 of these events spread across the United States, primarily in New England. In 1867, some groups joined to form the Associated Literary Society, which booked speakers on a singular, prescribed route from city to city across the country. This is the ubiquitous lecture circuit we hear people refer to all the time. Back then it was a singular thing you could get on. "Bye, honey, I'm going on the circuit...be back in six months," was something a famous lecturer might have said. It took that long to run the circuit across the country on horses and return home. Before the days of the Rolling Stones or U2, there were performers who survived the grueling months-long tours without double-decker tour buses, throngs of groupies, and all-hour parties.

---

3  In the interest of transparency and satisfying your curiosity, I average 25–30 lectures a year. Sometimes I'm paid as much as $8,000, depending on the situation. Maybe one-third are paid only in travel expenses or small fees, since they're self-promotional or for causes I'd like to help. Roughly 40% of my income is from book royalties and the rest from speaking and workshop fees. So far, I average around $100,000 a year, less than I made at Microsoft. However, I work fewer hours, am free from the 9 to 5 life, and have complete independence, which is worth infinitely more. I limit travel to once or twice a month, which means I turn away many gigs; I'd prefer to have more time than money, since you can never earn more time.

At first there was little money for speakers. The Lyceum was created as a public service, like an extension of your local library. It was a feel-good, grassroots, community-service movement aimed at educating people and popularizing ideas. These events were often free or inexpensive, such as 25 cents a ticket or $1.50 for an entire season.[4] But by the 1850s, when high-end speakers like Daniel Webster, Ralph Waldo Emerson, and Mark Twain dominated the circuit, prices for lectures went as high as $20 a ticket—equivalent to about $200 a seat in 2009. Of course, free lectures continued, and they always will, but the high end reached unprecedented levels for people giving speeches. In the late 1800s, it was something a famous person could do and earn more than enough money to make a comfortable living, which is exactly what many famous writers did.

Soon the free market took over. Air travel, radio, telephones, and everything else we take for granted today made the idea of a single circuit absurd. Lecture series, training conferences, and corporate meetings created thousands of events that needed new speakers every year. Some events don't pay, or even charge speakers to attend (as it's seen as an honor to be invited to give a presentation), but many hire a few speakers to ensure things go well. For decades, there's been enough demand for speakers that speaker bureaus—talent agencies for public speakers—work as middlemen, matching people who want to have a lecture at their event and speakers, like me, who wish to be paid for giving lectures. If you want Bill Clinton, Madonna, or Stephen King to speak at your birthday party, and you have the cash (see Table 3-1), there is a speaker bureau representing each one of them that would like to make a deal with you. Which brings us back to whether I'm worth $5,000.

*Table 3-1. High-end speakers and their fees.[a]*

| SPEAKER | ONE-HOUR LECTURE FEE |
| --- | --- |
| Bill Clinton | $150,000+ |
| Katie Couric | $100,000 |
| Malcolm Gladwell | $80,000 |
| Garry Kasparov | $75,000+ |

---

[4] *History of Public Speaking in America*, Robert T. Oliver (Allyn &Bacon), p. 461.

*Table 3-1. High-end speakers and their fees.[a] (continued)*

| Speaker | One-hour lecture fee |
|---------|---------------------|
| David Allen | $50,000–$75,000 |
| Ben Stein | $50,000–$75,000 |
| Wayne Gretsky | $50,000+ |
| Magic Johnson | $50,000+ |
| Bob Costas | $50,000+ |
| Maya Angelou | $50,000 |
| Rachel Ray | $50,000 |
| Dave Barry | $25,000–$30,000 |

[a] These fees were compiled from public listings on various speaker bureau websites. Most sites note that these fees are variable and may change at any time, and this list is a sample of the highest fees I could find. See *http://www.keyspeakers.com/* or *http://www.prosportspeaker.com/*.

My $5,000 fee has nothing to do with me personally. I'm not paid for being Scott Berkun. I know I'm paid only for the value I provide to whoever hires me. If, for example, my hosts can charge $500 per person for an event, and they get 500 people to attend, that's $250,000 in gross revenue. Part of what will allow them to charge that much, and draw that many people, is the speakers they will have. The bigger the names, the more prestigious their backgrounds, and the more interesting their presentations, the more people will come and the more they will be willing to pay.

Even for private functions—say, when Google or Ferrari throws an annual event for their employees—how much would it be worth to have a speaker who can make their staff a little smarter, better, or more motivated when returning to work? Maybe it's not worth $30,000 or even $5,000, but there is some economic value to what good speakers on the right topics do for people. It depends on how valuable the people in the room are to whoever is footing the bill. Even if it's just for entertainment, or for reminding the audience members of important things they've forgotten, a good speaker is worth something. Think of the last boring lecture you attended: would you have paid a few bucks to make the speaker suck less? I bet you would.

On the other hand, many events lose money. The high fixed costs of venue and food (the latter often heavily marked up by the former) make the event business more complex than it seems.

Often organizers must front all the money and hope attendance meets their break-even numbers. Many events make no profit at all, and understandably don't pay most of their speakers, as the goal is to serve their communities rather than to make revenue.[5] If you're thinking through all the places you've given a lecture, and feel angry you weren't paid, odds are good that no one was.

The disappointing thing is that even for high fees, speakers often don't do very well. After all, they're not being paid directly for their public-speaking skills. The raw economic value proposition is in drawing people to the event, and it's more likely that people will come to an event featuring a famous person—even one they suspect is boring to listen to—than to hear the best public speaker in the world (if that's his only claim to fame).[6] Two of the worst lectures I've attended were given by famous people: David Mamet (playwright, screenwriter, and director) and Nicholas Pileggi (author of *Wiseguy*, the novel Scorsese's *Goodfellas* was based on). Both occasions were author readings, which are notoriously boring and bad bets for good public speaking. Yet, in both cases, they filled their respective rooms impressively well. However, I bet no one in attendance got much from the experience of listening to them, except the right to say they saw a famous person speak, which perhaps is also worth something.

The challenge for event organizers, who have limited budgets and tough timelines, is to manage the three unavoidable criteria for picking people to talk at their events. They must find speakers who are:

1. Famous or credible for a relevant topic
2. Good at speaking
3. Available

Two out of three is often the best they can do. It's common to see good speakers who don't have much to say, as well as experts who are brilliant but boring. To secure someone with all three

---

[5] It would be nice if events explained where the profits go, if there are any. It's a good question to ask when invited to speak.

[6] There is an annual competition for the world's best public speaker, but I bet you've never heard of the winners: *http://www.toastmasters.org/Members/ MemberExperience/Contests/WorldChampions_1.aspx*.

often requires some cash, and as a result, I am one of thousands of people at the low end of a very high pay scale activity.

To put the numbers so far in this chapter in perspective, the average adult on planet Earth earns $8,200 a year (U.S. dollars), and the average American makes about $50,000.[7] Since you see your paycheck, you know exactly where you stand. I think it would be smart for corporations to put information like this on their checks—it would prevent many people from complaining about what they don't have.[8] Almost half of the world's population doesn't have clean running water or reliable electricity, no matter how well they are paid. From a planetary view, if you're reading this book indoors, under an electric light, within walking distance of a stocked refrigerator or a take-out delivery menu you can afford to order from, and rarely find yourself worrying about malaria or dysentery, you are doing quite well. And if you're still not happy, consider that compared to most of the galaxy, a place comprised of 99.9% dead, empty space, the fact you're even alive, and in the form of a species evolved enough to know you're alive, and educated enough to read books reminding you of how rare life is, makes you astronomically fortunate. We should be happy about this, but mostly it seems we're not.

Unfortunately, we know, care, and obsess more about the 10% of the world who earn more than we do than the 90% who earn less. And although you might disapprove of my speaking fees, I'm no different from you. I'm well aware of speakers who earn more than I do but who have less to say and say it worse than I would. It's safe to assume that no matter where you stand, someone would be happy to be in your shoes, just as you'd be happy to be in someone else's. I know all too well that rock stars, movie actors, Fortune 100 executives, and professional athletes make millions annually just for endorsing things they had nothing to do with. If I'm overpaid, at least it's to perform a service where I risk getting booed off the stage. An endorsement is paid for liking, or

---

7  See both *http://www.success-and-culture.net/articles/percapitaincome.shtml* and *http://www.census.gov/Press-Release/www/releases/archives/income_wealth/012528.html*.

8  I also think it would be good if salaries were made public, which is why I offered my fees and income. If more people did this, the overpaid and underpaid would be visible and more likely to be corrected. Or, total anarchy would ensue and civilization would end. Either way, it would be fun to watch.

merely pretending to like, something. It's not work in any familiar sense of the word, since it's a vague approval of work done by people the endorser has likely never met. Tiger Woods and LeBron James make more than $50 million a year from endorsements alone, an annual income so large it's more than the average American could earn in 10 lifetimes. This doesn't seem fair, and in a philosophical sense, it isn't. They are not doing anything for the greater good. They are not educating children, helping the poor, stopping wars, or curing diseases. In fact, depending on what they're endorsing, they're likely increasing our desire for what we don't have, can't afford, and probably don't need.

However, from another perspective, we all know people earn as much as they can argue for. If you're a fan of the free market, you must accept that if you feel underpaid, it's up to you to do something about it—the freest part of any market is *you*. You are free to quit and live in the woods like Thoreau, or to start your own business where you decide how much you're paid. For me, this means if I ever want to earn as much for a lecture as Bill Clinton or Bob Costas, I need to become way more famous by (in increasing order of desperation) writing better books, getting a better agent, or marrying Jessica Simpson. Of course, we are all free to complain about how unfair things are, as I am here. But let's be fair to people who earn more money than you think they should, including LeBron James, Tiger Woods, or even me. I bet if you picked an average American with an average job, and asked him using average language whether he'd rather be paid $100,000 instead of $50,000 for doing the same work, it's a safe bet that, on average, he'd say yes.

The only remaining defense for the speaker fees I'm paid is that I'm compensated for all the things everyone forgets I have to do in order to be capable of speaking. A keynote lecture to a large crowd takes about 60 minutes to deliver. Arguably this is more intense and stressful than the average office worker's entire week, but let's put that aside. To make and practice a new lecture takes two days of full-time work, which is 16 hours. Then consider my trip to get to the venue, including the security lines I have to wait in, the airplane flight I have to take, the cabs I have to ride in, the hotels I have to sleep in, and on it goes. Now, many people can give lectures, and I'm not being paid simply for talking into a microphone. I'm paid for the decades of experience listed on my resume that, in theory, should make what I have to say interesting, provocative, entertaining, educational, inspiring, and whatever other adjectives the people who hire me mention in their marketing material. I'm good at teaching, which is uncommon and worth a few bucks, but lastly there is the ultimate factor: I'm paid to speak at one venue instead of speaking at another. When demand outweighs supply, there are fees to be paid. The more demand, the higher the fees.

The unspoken risk I run is having no salary. I have no pension. I have no extended contract guaranteeing me lecture gigs forever. This book could bomb or be destroyed in reviews and my speaking career could come to an unfortunate and immediate end, which in the grand scheme of things would be OK. I didn't quit my job with the goal of earning $30,000 an hour—I quit to see if I could pull this off at all. And now that I have for the past five years, my goal is to see how long I can make an independent living purely on the merits of what I write and what I say.

## CHAPTER 4

# How to work a tough room

Half of what you pay for at a fancy restaurant isn't the food. You're paying its rent, you're paying for the atmosphere, and you're paying for the way its service makes you feel. If you've ever taken a date somewhere based on where it is, what it looks like, or how it feels to be there, you know this is true. Public speaking is no different; the atmosphere is important to the quality of everyone's experience. If you had to listen to Martin Luther King, Jr., in a New York City subway station, or Winston Churchill in a highway rest stop bathroom, with all the smells, noises, and rodents those atmospheric monstrosities are known for, you'd be less than pleased. MLK's most famous speech would go something like this: "I have a...<pauses as the A train speeds by at 110 decibels, audience covering their ears>...drea...oh, nevermind." His eloquence would be no match for the unpleasant and distractive powers of the environment around him. *Place* matters to a speaker because it matters to the audience. Old theaters, a university lecture hall, even the steps of the Lincoln Memorial are great places to speak, but most speakers rarely get asked to do their thing in venues this good. Most presentations are given under flickering fluorescent lights inside cramped conference rooms, or in convention halls designed with a thousand other functions in mind, which explains why I know way more than I should about chandeliers.

While you are in the audience looking up at the stage, a stage designed to make me easy to see, often I can't see anything (see Figure 4-1). All the house lights are aimed right at my face. People forget that the room, as bad as it might be, is set up to help the audience see, whereas we speakers are on our own. Whenever you see pictures of a famous person giving a famous lecture, you see the stage exactly the way the person with the best seat in the house saw it. No one else is on stage, and if someone is, he's not moving around. If President Obama were giving a speech and a dozen people behind him were eating cheeseburgers or playing charades, everyone in the audience would be quite annoyed. But when I look out into the audience, all I see are distractions. I can see and hear the back doors opening and closing with every person arriving late or leaving early. I see the glow of laptops in people's multitasking eyes. I see cameramen and stage crews moving heavy gear, flashing their lights, and making jokes, all in the back rows behind the crowd, where only I can see. And most

depressing of all, on some days, the days I forget to make a sacrifice to the gods of public speaking, all I can see when I look
straight ahead is the dizzying glare of the conference hall chandelier. These are the cheap ones, made of grey metal, covered in
chipping, peeling gold paint. They hover in the space above the
crowd, a place where few in the audience ever look, but precisely
where a speaker's eyes naturally want to go. In a good room, the
ceiling is free of distractions; in a bad room, there's a large
glowing ball of stupidity hanging there.

*Figure 4-1. At a big event with stage lights. This gives an idea of what I
see: mostly nothing.*

Disco balls work because they're undeniably silly and make fun of
real attempts at decoration, but chandeliers, even the cheap ones I
often see, are entirely serious. Despite their phony plastic flame-
shaped light bulbs (who was ever fooled by these?), they are a
lame attempt to give a room class, a kind of class that—to the disappointment of the owners of these rooms—cannot be obtained
by hanging something large and shiny from the ceiling. I'm told
these chandeliers are placed in conference halls for one reason: weddings. They want to rent the room out for weddings—the highest
marked-up events in the Western world—and somehow without an
ugly chandelier in the brochure, they fear they'll never be chosen as a
wedding venue again. Next time you're at a lecture, check the
ceiling. If you spot a chandelier, know that it's not there for you.

Why pick on a glorified light fixture? Why risk being banned from speaking at chandelier-industry conferences for the rest of my life? Here's why. Presenters talk about "tough rooms" all the time, usually referring to the audience. They blame the crowd when they should first blame the *room*. Many challenges are created by the room itself, challenges of atmosphere that change lukewarm crowds into tough ones. Ever try to throw a birthday party in a graveyard or a funeral in an amusement park? Of course not. You'd be set up to fail—unless your family has handfuls of Xanex for breakfast or you're related to Tim Burton. Most venues for speaking and lecturing in the modern world are dull, grey, uninspiring, poorly lit, generic cubes of space. They are designed to be boring (which is why it's hard to stay awake during lectures) so they can be used for anything. And like a Swiss Army knife, this means they suck at everything. Your average conference room or corporate lecture hall is bought and sold for its ability to serve many different purposes, though none of them well, which explains my unnatural, and possibly deadly, level of exposure to chandeliers. Blame speakers all you want—we do deserve most of the blame—but some fraction of hate should go to whoever chose the crappy room to stick the audience in. It's not my choice. If I had my choice, here's where you'd see me (check out Figure 4-2).

*Figure 4-2. The Greek Theater at Epidaurus.*

I'd want to be at this Greek amphitheater, in part, because I hear it's quite nice in Greece, but mostly because the ideal room for a lecture is a theater. It's crazy, I know, but we solved most lecture-room problems about 2,000 years ago. The Greek amphitheater gets it all just about right, provided it doesn't rain. Lecture rooms should be a semicircle, not a square. The stage should be a few feet higher than the front row, both to make people on the stage easier to see, but also to help them feel powerful. And most importantly, every row of seats should be higher off the ground than the one before it, giving everyone a clear line of sight. All of these things make it easier for the audience to stay interested and focus its attention on center stage, as well as provide the speaker with natural acoustics.

One of the best lectures I've given in recent memory was at Carnegie Mellon University in the Adamson Wing, a theater-sized room that seats maybe 120 (see Figure 4-3).[1] If you put a kegerator inside the lectern and added a remote-controlled shock system that would electrify individual seats on command (an anti-heckler device), it would be perfect.

**Figure 4-3.** *The Adamson Wing at Carnegie Mellon University, a room designed well for lectures.*

---

[1] As an alumni of Carnegie Mellon University, I got a special thrill from speaking in a room I'd fallen asleep in many times. However, the bigger rooms in Doherty Hall should be studied for their sleep-inducing powers.

And, of course, the most overlooked advantage of Greek-style amphitheaters and good university lecture halls? No chandeliers.

Theaters are rare. They cost more to build and to rent, and few conference centers have them. When they do, they're often reserved for the big-name speakers on the schedule. Everyone else gets the square, dingy, poorly lit loser rooms. I speak in loser rooms all the time. But if you're invited to give a lecture and get a choice of rooms, ask for the one that's most theater-like. Even if it's smaller, even if it's farther away, the room will score you extra points. I get giddy all over when I know I'm speaking in a room set up to help me connect with the audience. A room free of poles and blind spots, a room with good lighting, a room that's sound-proofed well enough so we don't hear the traffic outside or the lecture next door. It's rare, but when it happens, the people who hire me get their money's worth.

In a square room, there are many problems few talk about. If you're in an aisle seat at the far right or left of the room, staring straight ahead, you'll be looking at the front wall. To see what's going on, you have to turn your head or your body toward the center of the front. You also have to try and look over or between the heads of the people in front of you—which if you're more than 20 rows back can be impossible. If you can't see the speaker, why are you there? You might as well watch the lecture on TV in the bar, so you can play lecture drinking games with your friends, such as "ummmster," where you do a shot of your favorite cocktail every time the speaker says "ummm." With some speakers, you'll be passed out in no time.

If you're in the audience, the angle of your body and the amount of eye contact you make with the speaker might not seem to affect your quality of experience, but for the speaker, it does. When 50, 100, or 5,000 people can give 10% more of their attention and energy to you—whether through their eye contact, posture, or laughter—it makes the difference between feeling confident and feeling lost. One extra pair of friendly eyes, or the visibility of an affirmative nod now and then, changes how any speaker feels. And in a good room—whether you're at a concert or presentation— energy moves easily between the crowd and the stage.

Even in bad clubs, musicians have many advantages for controlling the energy in a room—bass drums and amplified guitars literally force waves of energy to bounce around, getting people to
dance or respond in various other ways. But in a grey, boring
square room of right angles on top of right angles—where half the
crowd mostly sees the bald spots in the hairlines of the people sitting in front of them, and where instead of a bass drum, they hear
the whiny voice of, for example, the head of accounting droning
on about the right way to fill out page 9, section F of the new
expense reports—the energy in the room is split and fractured well
before it leaves the stage. It bounces around, gets eaten by the
walls, drained by the dull carpet, smothered by the dim lights, and
dies. A speaker, unarmed with a guitar or bongos, is on his own to
overcome the deficiencies of the space. Even good speakers are frequently eaten alive by the effects of bad rooms.

The worst situation, even worse than being in a bad room, is
being in a big, bad empty room. Speaking in a huge, boring, rectangular, dimly lit room that seats 1,000 people is challenging
enough, but with only 100 attendees present, these rooms feel like
black holes. Even if you're screaming, dancing, and juggling
knives, it may not be possible to generate enough energy to fill the
space. I once saw U2 play at the Meadowlands in New Jersey,
which holds 60,000 people. By the end of the show, people were
streaming out to beat the traffic, and no matter what Bono did on
stage, the stadium was dead. There were still 20,000 dancing people
there, but it seemed like the lamest 20,000 people I'd ever seen.

A related personal disaster took place when I spoke at Microsoft's
Tech-Ed conference in Dallas in 1998. I drew the short straw: I
had the largest room of the entire massive hotel conference center
complex. The ceilings were so high, and the back wall was so distant from the stage, that I actually asked the tech crew if it was a
converted aircraft hangar. It must have been used for something
other than training events. There was no reason for this room to
have the scale it did, other than to torture public speakers. The crew
looked up at the ceiling when I asked, and were sort of surprised
there was a ceiling there at all. They never thought to look up, as
they spend most of their time just trying to fix all the stuff that
breaks down at ground level. I should have told them about how
stars hover in the night sky—it would have blown their minds.

The room was set with chairs for over 2,000 people. When I heard this, my ego lit up: 2,000 people? To see me? Wow. I must be super cool. But as the countdown timer ticked away—20 minutes, 10 minutes, 5—and I'd spent all that time staring out at a sea of empty seats, I was mortified. I didn't want to go on. I'd never seen so many empty chairs all in one place. Where did they keep them? There must have been a huge storeroom just for these chairs. How utterly pathetic for someone to have spent an afternoon arranging them all, only for those chairs to sit empty and unloved. And how depressing that I was the person who had failed to fill them.

With a minute to go, a few people were seated here and there. A handful more walked in from the back exit, like little ants entering my zip code–sized room (you always get a few at the last minute). It was nice to see them, but they quickly disappeared into the cave-like darkness between the aisles. With 20 seconds to go, I noticed one guy up front, finally aware of the tumbleweeds drifting past him, grab his things and scurry toward the door. So much for him. Five seconds. The house lights came up and with them came a wave of heat over my face and arms. The few pairs of eyes in the room were now all on me. It was time to start.

What could I do? Was there anything that could be done? My body chose to panic. Having panicked before, I knew the only trick was to start, as fear comes from what you imagine might happen instead of what actually is happening, and the longer you wait, the worse it gets. The only way to kill this evil feedback loop is to just do it, so I forced myself to begin. And I sucked. For an hour I sucked—an endless hour of misery, speaking into the Grand Canyon of rooms, with each and every word traveling slowly across a sea of empty chairs. I heard every word twice, once when I said it, and two seconds later when it echoed against the back wall, unimpeded by the sound-absorbing powers of an actual crowd. When I finished, I sulked my way to a dark corner of the hotel bar, hid behind a row of beers, and hoped not to be seen.

The solution to this, and to many other tough room problems, rests on the density theory of public speaking, a theory I discovered one day after repeating the Dallas experience in some other city, with some other embarrassingly small crowd in a ridiculously large room. I realized that the crowd size is irrelevant—what matters is having a *dense* crowd. If ever you face a sparsely populated audience, do whatever you have to do to get them to move together. You want to create a packed crowd located as close as possible to the front of the room. This goes against most speakers' instincts, which push them to just go on with the show and pretend not to notice it feels like they're speaking at the Greyhound bus station at 3 a.m. on Christmas morning.

Those few people in the audience know as well as you do that the room is empty, and if you act like you don't notice, they'll know you're full of shit before you get five minutes into your talk. Audiences, even tough crowds, genuinely want to help you, but no one in the audience can do anything about bad energy. Only two people in the room have that control: the host and the speaker. The host, a person who likely knows little about public speaking (much less the density theory), and who probably has 25 other event problems more important than your empty room, is unlikely to be of use. Hell, he chose to put you in the room of certain death to begin with. So all hope rests in the hands of whoever has the microphone, and that's you (see Figure 4-4).

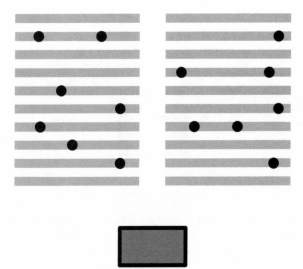

*Figure 4-4. A small crowd in a big room. Your energy can never effectively reach everyone because it will be eaten by all the dead space.*

Forty-five people in a 2,000-person room is not a crowd, it's the equivalent devastation of a neutron bomb. This means the first move is to forget the 2,000 seats. Forget the empty rows and dead spaces.

Imagine a smaller room inside the big one that seats about 50 people (see Figure 4-5). Make the room your own by asking the attendees to gather into that more intimate space. If you leave them scattered in the wasteland of empty seats, they will feel like lonely losers. They will feel embarrassed for having chosen to come see you instead of any of a thousand other nonembarrassing things they could have done with their hour. If you pack them together, at least they'll know they're not the only losers who decided to come hear you. They are now losers with loser friends, which—all things considered—is much better than being a loser without any friends at all. They are, in fact, your losers, so you should treat them well.

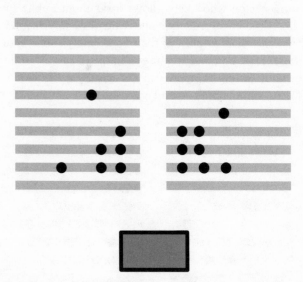

**Figure 4-5.** *A properly arranged small crowd in a big room. You can do good work here despite the empty space.*

The tricky part is getting people to move. We are a lazy species. I know once I'm seated I'm not very interested in getting up just to sit down again. But the fact is, all of us do what people in authority tell us to do, especially in lecture halls. We have spent our lives listening to people at the front of crowded rooms telling us to stand up, sit down, sing songs, close our eyes, play "Simon Says," repeat national anthems, and a thousand other stupid things we'd never agree to do if we weren't being dictated to by someone with a microphone. It doesn't matter where you are or how scared the crowd suspects you might be, if you have the mike and explain the situation with a smile, when you ask them nicely to stand up and move forward, they will. Make it a game. Offer a prize to the person who gets up first. Ask the audience members if they need more exercise today, and when they all raise their hands (people who go to lectures and conferences always crave exercise), tell them you have just the thing for them to do. You might eat a few minutes of your time, but it's worth it if you have a long session. And whoever speaks to the same crowd after you will be grateful.

The few that don't oblige should be left in the back of the room anyway. There's no law stating that you must treat everyone in the audience the same. Give preferential treatment to the people who respond to your requests. By making them move, you've done a few other beneficial things. They've now invested something in you, and you will have their attention for at least the next two minutes. You spoke the truth about the uncomfortable nature of the room, and people will respect your honesty and willingness to take action to fix it. And for your sake, you've identified the leaders and fans: they're the ones who got up first. These are the people most interested in you and what you have to say. If there are any allies in the crowd—the people first to applaud or ask a question—you now know who they are.

Most importantly, the density theory amplifies your energy. We're social creatures. If five people—or even dogs, raccoons, or other social animals—get together, they start to behave in shared ways. They make decisions together, they move together, and most importantly, they become a kind of short-term community. With a tightly packed crowd, if I make one person laugh, nod his head, or smile, the people directly adjacent will notice and be slightly more prone to do it themselves. TV sitcoms have laugh tracks for this reason: we respond to what the crowd around us is doing. Even simply having the woman next to you listening with her full attention changes the atmosphere for the better, versus sitting next to an annoying dude checking his email who doesn't look up once. The size of the room or the crowd becomes irrelevant as long as the people there are together in a tight pack, experiencing and sharing the same thing at the same time.

There are many similar adjustments a speaker can make to a room. Turn up the lights if it feels like you're in a cave. Ask for a wireless microphone or bring your own if you hate being tied to the lectern. If you spot someone stuck behind a pole or standing in the back, offer him a seat near the front that he might not have noticed was empty. Always travel with a remote for your laptop so you can move to a better spot if the lectern was placed in some stupid back corner of the stage. Ask the crowd if they're too cold or too warm, and then, on the mike, ask the organizers to do something about it (even if they can't, you look great by being the only speaker to give a care about how the audience is feeling). There are always little things you can do—that don't require the construction of your own private lecture theater—to improve how the room feels. When you have the microphone, it's your room— do whatever you'd like to enhance the audience's experience.

Failing to own your turf is the big mistake that can create a tough crowd. If I show up five minutes before I start speaking, I have no idea what the vibe is like. Every audience is different for a thousand reasons, from what the traffic was like that morning to what sports team won or lost the night before to what community politics are happening. If I just show up right before my talk, I can't sort out how much of it has to do with me as opposed to general hatred for the world at large. Taking responsibility for the crowd means showing up to the room early enough to at least hear the previous speaker. Sometimes you'll hear a joke or comment in the previous talk that you can pick up on, or know to avoid, given that it's been used before. If the speaker was awesome but only got cold stares from the crowd, you know something is up that's larger than you or the other speaker. But if he does well and gets great energy and strong applause, yet you go down in flames, you know it's not the audience—it's you.

Speaking in foreign countries makes this all too clear. You have no idea what a tough crowd is until you've spoken in Sweden, Japan, or scores of other countries where laughing, joking, and yelling out support during a presentation are cultural taboos. And unless you speak the local language, you're being translated, which means the audience doesn't know what you said—or what the translator decided you said—until about 10 seconds after you've said it. When I spoke in Moscow, live translated just like at the United Nations, the audience was awesome, but I didn't know why they were laughing until the translator explained it through my earpiece. For long, horrible moments, I was afraid they were laughing at or heckling me, rather than supporting what I'd said. After speaking through live translation a few times, presenting to a rowdy crowd is a breeze if they speak your native language.

If all else fails—you know the audience hates you and your point of view—seek out the person who hates you the least. All rooms, no matter how tough, have one person who hates you the least. Even if you're a Flying Spaghetti Monster disciple speaking at the Vatican, someone in that room will hate you less than everyone else.[2] Maybe it's because he thinks you're cute or he's amused by how scared you are to be there, but he's your best chance. If you are going to get a first smile, a nod of support, or a round of applause, it's going to come from him. Once you find that one person, use him as your base. Don't ignore everyone else, but know where to look for support. Or, if you arrive early, take the initiative to talk to people in the crowd and find some supporters. Ask them to move up front. Alternatively, you might discover the one person who has a really good reason to hate you and make sure not to let him ask the first question during Q&A.

Sometimes the tough crowd is entirely imagined and then created by the speaker, who, realizing the audience is hostile, blames them. What kind of idiot does this sort of thing? My kind of idiot. The first big lecture I gave was in 1996. It was an internal lecture at Microsoft to about 200 engineers and managers. At the arrogant age of 24, I was so certain the crowd would tear me to pieces that I made sure they never had a chance. I spoke in my fastest New-Yorker-who-wants-to-kick-your-ass tone, never smiled, and made clear my unwillingness to let anyone in the audience enjoy anything from the moment I opened my mouth. Why did I do all this? Why did I come off so unpleasant? I was terrified. And as an arrogant and frightened young man, I took it out on the people I most feared. I watched the video of this talk and destroyed it afterward. That's how ridiculous my behavior was.

In the act of protecting myself from what I thought would be a hostile, critical, skeptical audience, I set about on the one course

---

2  For information on the Church of the Flying Spaghetti Monster, see *http://www. venganza.org/about/*.

most likely to create the thing I was trying to avoid. I'm sure this happens often: being paranoid has strikingly good odds of creating what we're afraid of, perpetuating the paranoia. If I hadn't later seen that video of my performance, I wouldn't have the life I have now. I would always have thought I was responding to the crowd, not that *it was responding to me*. I would have continually wondered why my crowds were so unpleasant, and eventually given up. Now I know I have to embody what I want the audience to be. If I want them to have fun, I have to have fun. If I want them to laugh, I have to laugh. But it has to be done in a way they can connect with, which is hard to do. A drunken toast at a wedding is often great fun for the toaster but miserable for everyone else. But great speakers are connection-makers, sharing an authentic part of themselves to create a singular, positive experience for the audience.

One unusual way to think about tough crowds is that a crowd has to be interested in you to hate you. A hostile crowd gives you more energy to work with than an indifferent one. Giving a lecture to a room full of people in comas, literally in hospital beds, wired up to IVs filled with various horse tranquilizers, has a zero percent chance of them being interested in you. But if people are angry or rowdy, it means they care about something. They have some energy they are willing to contribute, for better or for worse. If you can figure out what it is they're interested in, preferably early on, it's possible to connect with them. Find common ground and bring it to the surface. Their hate will quickly turn to respect, as you've said the thing on stage they've never heard someone like you say before. After watching and giving hundreds of lectures, I've learned that by far the thing people seem angriest about is dishonesty. Show some integrity by speaking the truth on the very thing that angers them, or even acknowledging it in a heartfelt way, and you will score points. People with the courage to speak the truth into a microphone are exceptionally rare.

Few people know that Dale Carnegie's most popular book, *How to Win Friends & Influence People* (Pocket), which is one of the bestselling self-help books in history, received significant backlash from the press and cultural elites of its time. Carnegie was ridiculed in editorials and cartoons, and mocked at colleges and universities, for offering over-simplified and sappy advice (in the same way Deepak Chopra and Dr. Phil are made fun of today).

He was invited to speak at the Dutch Treat Club in New York City, an elite group of publishers, editors, and advertising men, the kind of cynical, tough-minded folks most critical of his work. Despite warnings from his advisors, he chose to speak anyway, and here's what he said:

> *I know there's considerable criticism of my book. People say I'm not profound and there's nothing in it new to psychology and human relations. This is true. Gentlemen, I've never claimed to have a new idea. Of course I deal with the obvious, I present, reiterate, and glorify the obvious—because the obvious is what people need to be told. The greatest need of people is to know how to deal with other people. This should come naturally to them, but it doesn't. I am told that you are a hostile audience. But I plead "not guilty." The ideas I stand for are not mine. I borrowed them from Socrates. I swiped them from Chesterfield. I stole them from Jesus, and I put them in a book. If you don't like their rules, whose would you use? I'd be glad to listen.[3]*

According to one report, he received a huge round of applause. While I'm not a big fan of that book, I am a fan of this story. He handled a tough crowd in a bold, smart, and honest way.

However, on some days, no matter what you do, some folks will hate you anyway. Occasionally, I encounter people who love to hate, or I just rub them the wrong way for reasons I can't explain. I once had a professor at a university I was invited to lecture at interrupt me three times before I moved past my first slide. Minutes later, after long glares and inventively loud sighs, he got up and left.[4] Could I have done anything differently? I didn't think so. Sometimes a person just doesn't like you and takes pleasure in hating you. If I had tried to please him, perhaps I'd just make someone else equally mad. I don't mind being hated, since I hate some things and people, too. But when it disrupts the audience, it's now ruining something the rest of the room seems to enjoy. Once the professor left, he spared me the challenge of having to ask him to shut up or leave, which I would have had to do if he continued.

---

3 From *The Man Who Influenced Millions*, Giles Kemp and Edward Claflin (St. Martin's Press), p. 154.

4 After the lecture, his students apologized for his behavior; apparently, I was not the first to be received so warmly. I politely contacted him afterward to see what he was upset about. His response was to offer to send me some of his books so I "might learn something."

For that, perhaps I should be grateful. It's easy to forget that most people feel trapped in their seats. If they want to leave, they can't bear the attention they'd get for standing up and scrambling over people's knees to get to the aisle. If someone is unhappy, I'm happy to see him go rather than spoil the energy for everyone else. I don't find it rude at all—it's a blessing. A small crowd of 5 interested people looks bad but is a better situation than 50 people who want to leave but won't.

If you're truly afraid you will be on hostile turf, some extra legwork can relieve your fears. Ask your host how large the crowd tends to be and what common questions might get asked. Request the names of three people to interview who are representative of the crowd you will speak to. See if your fears are real or imagined. Then, when giving your talk, make sure to mention, "Here are the three top complaints I heard from my research with Tyler, Marla, and Cornelius." Including the audience in your talk will score you tons of points. Few people ever do this, and if the rest of the crowd disagrees with Tyler, Marla, or Cornelius, they can sort that out on their own after you leave.

## CHAPTER 5

# Do not eat the microphone

There are many stupid people in this world, and I'm sure you've met some of them. George Carlin, one of the brightest minds of our time, once observed that the average person isn't that smart—and worse, half the population is dumber than that average person. More interesting perhaps is whenever I ask a room full of people, "Who here thinks they're above average intelligence?", more than half the room always raises their hands. If you are truly smarter than those around you, your superiority should make you feel good; but then again, even the smart among us do stupid things. Einstein flunked his college entrance exams just as Julius Caesar overlooked the pointy knives in his friends' robes. I'm sure Mozart spilled coffee on his piano and Julia Child burned Thanksgiving turkeys now and then. All considered, given the vast number of stupid people—and bright people doing stupid things—in the world, some public speakers will seem less than smart. There is no way around it. No amount of training will make a man with two brain cells seem anything but dumb, as the problem is not his ability to speak, it's his inability to think. It's rarely said, but some people will never be good public speakers. Unless they find someone to do their thinking for them, they only have, at best, half the tools they need.

Even for many smart people working on a presentation, they're so seduced by style that they lose the substance. They worry about slide templates, images, movies, fonts, clothes, hair, and the rest, forgetting to do the harder and more important work of thinking deeply about what points they want to make. It is possible to become an eloquent speaker, who makes beautiful slides and has a great vocabulary and perfect diction, without having much to say. Or worse, has much to say that is untrue, misleading, and impractical for or irrelevant to the audience. I wouldn't call these people idiots precisely, but it would be fair to say they've squandered much of their brain's energy considering problems that were not the most important to solve. The problem with most bad presentations I see is not the speaking, the slides, the visuals, or any of the things people obsess about. Instead, it's the lack of thinking.

There are many things that get in the way of good thinking, but the legend that Lincoln wrote the Gettysburg Address on the back of an envelope is especially notorious for doing so. The story is often told to suggest Lincoln's brilliance—that he could just scribble one of the greatest speeches of all time in a few spare moments while riding on a train. It's a story that inspires many to forgo preparing in favor of getting up on stage and winging it, as if that's what great leaders and thinkers do. The fallacy of the legend is to assume that the only moments Lincoln spent thinking about the points he would make in the speech took place as he wrote them. That somehow he never thought about the horrors of the Civil War, the significance of human sacrifice, and the future of the United States except while he wrote down the words of the address on a random scrap of paper. The anecdote is so charming that few consider the years he spent thinking about these complex issues, the lengthy debates he had with peers and rivals, and the stacks of speeches and letters he wrote on these subjects, all of which helped him refine his thoughts and clarify his points.

If it matters any, the story of the envelope is probably a myth. Dale Carnegie, who spent many years studying Lincoln, has this to say about the making of the Gettysburg Address:[1]

> *He (Lincoln) was spending the later part of that evening giving his speech "another lick." He even went to an adjoining house where Secretary Seward was staying and read the speech aloud to him for criticism. After breakfast the next morning he continued to give it "another lick," working on it until a tap came at the door telling him to take his place in the procession.*

All good public speaking is based on good private thinking. JFK, for all his brilliance, had speechwriters, who likely penned his famous quote, "Ask not what your country can do for you, ask what you can do for your country."[2] Same is true for Ronald Reagan, Barack Obama, most CEOs, and many of the most famous public speakers throughout history. Much of what these speechwriters do is transform a rough set of ideas into clear points. This means the difference between you and JFK or Martin Luther King has less to do with your ability to speak—a skill all of us use hundreds of times every day—than it does the ability to think and refine rough ideas into clear ones. Making a point,

---

1 *Public Speaking for Success*, Dale Carnegie (Arthur Pell), p. 32.

2 It's not clear whether JFK or his speechwriters intentionally echoed previous speeches, but others had said much the same thing. For example, "We pause to ask what our country has done for each of us and to ask ourselves what we can do for our country in return," spoken by Oliver Wendell Holmes on May 30, 1884. This mild restating and reuse of other people's ideas in speeches is common (as is misquoting).

teaching a lesson, or conveying a feeling to others first requires thinking, lots and lots of thinking, before the speaking ever happens. But we don't see the thinking; after all, it's not very interesting to watch. We only see the speaking, which makes it seem as though the thinking magically happened all by itself.

No matter what kind of speaking you are doing, there are only a few reasons people will be there. As you plan your talk, start with the goal of satisfying the things listed below. People come because they:

1.  Want to learn something
2.  Wish to be inspired
3.  Hope to be entertained
4.  Have a need they hope you will satisfy
5.  Desire to meet other people interested in the subject
6.  Seek a positive experience they can share with others
7.  Are forced to be there by their bosses, parents, professors, or spouses
8.  Have been handcuffed to their chairs and haven't left the room for days

Only a fool can talk for an hour and completely miss them all. Many talks hit one or two of these at least by accident. However, a thoughtful speaker—a speaker without extraordinary eloquence or magic powers but who cares deeply about giving the audience something of use—can talk for 30 minutes, nail most of the first six, and end early, setting everyone free and having satisfied all of those in attendance (including those in the room for reasons seven and eight).

Many speakers at conferences provide bios explaining in detail how great they are at running companies, managing teams, getting degrees, or writing books, all evidence to support the claim that they are good at doing things for other people. If speakers are as smart and talented as their resumes claim, we should expect them to take seriously the reasons people are in the room listening to them. But since they're presenting, and they have the microphone, they allow themselves to become the center of attention, forgetting where their priorities should be.

Put another way, when 100 people are listening to you for an hour, that's 100 hours of people's time devoted to what you have to say. If you can't spend 5 or 10 hours preparing for them, thinking about them, and refining your points to best suit their needs, what does that say about your respect for your audience's time? It says that your 5 hours are more important than 100 of theirs, which requires an ego larger than the entire solar system. And there is no doubt this disrespect will be obvious once you are on the stage.

In February 2009, at a major conference, I watched a famous executive give a lecture to a crowd of hundreds of people. Minutes into his presentation, he fell into a sea of silence, flipped through the papers in his hand, and finally confessed that he was confused by his own notes.[3] This was because he had stopped following them minutes before; flustered, he apologized and said he would never do this again. What he discovered, and explained to the audience, was that he found it impossible to speak extemporaneously and use notes at the same time. His entire speech was 20 minutes long, so if he had spent 20 minutes practicing in the weeks before the event, he could have figured out just how impossible it was to do this before he ever got on stage. This would have helped him understand the key points he wanted to make, saving the entire paying audience from using its time to help him figure it all out.

Audiences are very forgiving. They want the speaker to do well, so they will overlook many superficial problems. But if the speaker is not going to think carefully about his points, willfully disregards his own material, and gets lost as a result, how forgiving can the audience be? In most professional situations, such unpreparedness would be unacceptable. Imagine if a doctor stopped midway through your brain surgery and asked you to remind him of the goal of the surgery. If you don't know why you're on the stage, the audience cannot help you.

In the speaking trade, this is known as *eating the microphone*. It's the moment when the audience's confidence in having its needs met is lost. Everyone stops listening. This never happens because of typos, bad slides, or even a momentarily confused speaker. It happens when the speaker wanders far away from anything the

---

[3] There is nothing wrong with having or mentioning notes, provided the talk you give is good.

audience cares about. When this happens, it's understood that it's OK to daydream, play Solitaire on cell phones, or simply get up and leave—people know they will make better use of their time than the speaker will.

When a fool eats the microphone, it might be a good thing. But it is a tragedy when a smart, interesting person, with great stories and insights to share, fails an audience due to lack of forethought. The potential for all the good things in the aforementioned list was in the room that day—a thousand possible connections of people and ideas and passions—but it was squandered because he forgot about the audience. My point isn't even about practice; although it's important, it's not sufficient since anyone can throw hours at a problem and still stink. The goal is to use your preparation time so your thinking is strong, making it easy to satisfy most audiences despite any mistakes that might happen when you get on stage.

To prepare well, you must do four things:

1.  **Take a strong position in the title.** All talks and presentations have a point of view, and you need to know what yours is. If you don't know enough about the topic to have an opinion, solve that problem before you make your presentation. Even saying, "Here are five things I like" is a strong position, in that there are an infinite number of things you did not choose. With a weak position, your talk may become, "Here is everything I know I could cram into the time I have, but since I have no idea if you care, or what I would say if I had less time to talk, you get a half-baked, hard to follow, hard to present, pile of trash." Whenever I see a bored speaker, I want to ask him: "What is the talk you really wanted to give?" or "What did you really want to say?" For some reason, it seems he didn't think he was allowed to give that talk, a talk the audience probably came to hear.

2.  **Think carefully about your specific audience.** Know why they are there, what their needs are, what background knowledge they have, the pet theories they believe in, and how they hope their world will be different after your lecture is over. If you don't have time to study your subject, at least study your audience. It may turn out that as little as you know about a subject, you know more about it than your audience.

3. **Make your specific points as concise as possible.** If it takes 10 minutes to explain what your point is, something is very wrong. Points are claims. Arguments are what you do to support your points. Every point should be compressed into a single, tight, interesting sentence. The arguments might be long, but no one should ever be confused as to what your point is while you are arguing it. A mediocre presentation makes the points clear but muddles or bores people with the arguments. A truly bad presentation never clarifies what the points are.

4. **Know the likely counterarguments from an intelligent, expert audience.** If you do not know the intelligent counterarguments to each of your points, your points cannot be good. For example, if your presentation is about why people should eat more cheese, you should at a minimum know why the Anti-Cheese Foundation of America[4] says people should eat less cheese.

The fastest way to achieve these things is to start with a strong title. Titles get so little attention, but they're always the first words on your slides. And if you're speaking at an event or conference, it's how people choose whether they want to attend your session. Most people pick boring, lifeless titles for their presentations. This is a spectacular disaster of lost opportunity. A title divides the universe into what you will talk about and what you won't. There are a million ways to do this, but most of them are boring. If you can't figure out a smart way to divide up the topic, odds are poor that you'll find useful points to make. If you had only one single point, what would it be? That's what your title should communicate.

Even if you must have a boring title because your boss forces you to, don't use the boring title at the beginning. Choose a working title that you think your audience really wants to hear, or that strongly represents what you have to say. Status presentations, where people give updates on their work, are a tragedy because everyone hates how boring everyone else's is, but refuses to do something smarter in their own presentations. If you call yours something like, "The good, the bad, and what we're doing about it," the conciseness of your presentation and the value of the meetings in general would improve dramatically.

---

4 This is a fictitious organization, so don't bother searching for it on the Web. Or perhaps if you have anti-cheese rage, now's the time to start the group yourself.

Here's a better example. Say I agree to give a lecture entitled "Creativity for beginners." I have already set myself up to fail. How can I possibly say everything a beginner needs to know about creativity? And why would the audience care to know everything? That would be boring and take forever. Good lectures are never comprehensive because it's the wrong format to do so. I might as well read the dictionary to someone for six hours—it would be just as ineffective. People really want insight. They want an angle. A good speaker or teacher finds it for them.

A better title would be, "How to be creative in doing boring work" or "Green eggs and brainstorming: how to learn creativity from reading Dr. Seuss." Even if I used a worn-out, beaten-to-death generic title like, "Instant creativity in five minutes a day," from the moment I started working on the presentation, I would know what the value is for the audience. I'd be cleanly defining what I am covering and what I am not covering. This sets up any speaker on any topic to succeed. By slicing the topic in a specific and interesting way, all thinking that follows will be easier, more fun, and more likely to be relevant to the people who show up.

But speakers don't like interesting titles because, well, I'm not sure why. For some it's a reflection of their general fears of speaking. The craving for safety is so strong that they're compelled to follow the same recipe that's put us to sleep a thousand times. They put in all the facts, jargon, and diagrams they can manage, never really intending to clearly say anything (in the hopes of preventing anyone from asking a decent question). Consider a talk titled, "Risk management 101." For those who remember college, 101 courses were boring. They're often designed to put people to sleep rather than excite them. And worse, intro college courses are generally taken because they are required, not desired. Naming a talk "<Insert thing here> 101" in the hopes of making it attractive, denies how boring most 101 courses in the history of the universe have been for students.

Take a simple title like, "The five biggest questions and answers you have about X." I'm convinced you could find any reasonably intelligent person, drop him into any organization in the world with the assignment of making this presentation, and he'd do a decent job. Even if he knows nothing about X, he can research people in the appropriate audience, find out their questions, seek out good answers from experts in the company, and present them. It's always possible to do some kind of research on the people likely to attend a presentation, and it makes sorting out what direction to go in more substantiated than just guessing. If you think of a presentation as a kind of product, customer research makes sense. There's no law stopping you from studying the kind of people you expect will listen to you and aiming your material at what they want to hear.

You can rip off any of the following titles and be well on your way to a stronger presentation:

- The top five problems you have with <insert thing here> and how to solve them
- Why <insert thing here> sucks and what we can do about it
- Mistakes I made in <insert thing here> and what I learned
- The most frequently asked questions and brilliant answers about <insert thing here>
- The truth about <insert thing here> and how it can help you
- Smart shortcuts and clever tricks only experts know about <insert thing here>
- The five reasons you win by giving me <insert thing here>
- Why <insert thing here> will change your life forever, for free, right now

With an interesting title, even one you're not sure you can live up to, the work shifts to possible points that just might fulfill what the title is promising. Grab a piece of paper and brainstorm by listing all the thoughts you have on the topic, even the strange, half-baked ones.

Let's assume I chose the title, "How eating cheese will save your life." (Even though this is a bizarre topic, one I've never thought about, it's a useful exercise to show—without even doing much research—how easy it is to develop the seeds for an interesting talk.) My list might look something like this:

- Cheese tastes good. (Who doesn't like cheese? My uncle hates cheese. How can I find out what percentage of people don't like cheese at all?)
- It has fun names that make you laugh (Havarti, Munster, and Manchego!).
- Cheesemonger. Also fun to say.

- It's high in calcium and other vitamins. (Is this true? What about high fat?)

- People need to enjoy their food and enjoy life...hedonism can be good. (Has cheese ever killed anyone? Are there cheese fatalities? Death by cheese? Why does Swiss cheese have holes in it? Swiss cheese looks sort of like a cheese grater, which is odd. What happens if you try to grate Swiss cheese? Can't be good. Must find out.)

- To learn about cheese is to learn about food. (This sounds phony. When did people start saying "cheesy" to mean phony?)

- American cheese is a travesty. Who came up with Velveeta? Velvet and food do not mix. And what about that plastic yellow stuff they pour on nachos at movie theaters?

- Macaroni and cheese. Why is it so popular in the U.S.? Was it popular before Kraft? Why doesn't anyone seem upset by Kraft's monopoly on macaroni and cheese?

- What about lactose intolerance? What do I say to those people?

- Can people get good cheese mail-order? Are there Internet resources on why to love cheese and how to get it?

With a title and list in hand, you now have a *strawman*: a rough sketch of what your talk might cover and the points it might make. Show it to coworkers, friends, or even potential audience members, and ask them how to make the list better. If you have no friends and all your coworkers hate you, do some web searches. Flesh out your list; add more questions and ideas. Don't worry about how to support the points, answer the questions, or even whether you entirely agree with them. Just make a big, long, and most important of all, interesting list. A dozen is good, 15 is brilliant, and 20 makes you a rock star. In all cases, put the list aside, pat yourself on the back, and go have a beer. That's right, walk away and do something completely unrelated to your talk or your list.

This sounds ridiculous since you're probably overdue for your slides or you waited too long to read this chapter (in which case you should switch from reading this book to drinking beers). But if you want your talk to be good, you must let your list breathe. Get some distance so that when you return to it, you can critique the list not like the person who's proud to have just written down some points, but like the smarter, less patient guy who will be in your audience. Review, improve, and repeat.

Eventually, reorder the list from top to bottom in terms of how strongly you feel about each point. You might find that two cancel each other out or one is really a subpoint of another. Perhaps you'll realize there is a better title than the one you started with. Fine, change it. You should know much more about your topic now than when you started, so reflect that in the position your title takes.

With enough effort, you'll settle down to a list of five strong, interesting, reasonably aligned points, as well as a bunch of weird, mangled, half-baked stuff. If there's a cliff in quality between the good stuff and the half-baked, draw a line to make it clear. In my wacky example, my list for "How eating cheese can save your life" would look something like this:

1. Cheese is universal. (It's been around for 4,000 years. It's organic, natural. Are there any cultures that don't eat cheese? Any that don't drink milk?)

2. America has bad cheese history and cheese stigma. (Travesties include Velveeta, American cheese, and that weird, plastic-looking, paint-like, noncheese substance that is served on nachos at movie theaters. How did this happen? Is there a bad-cheese conspiracy?)

3. Cheese is among the most flavorful and diverse foods ever (5,000 different uses, a zillion[5] different kinds, melted/non-melted, etc.).

4. Cheesemongers are local experts and can pair a cheese with any meal. (Bonus points if you like wine—even more pairings and explosions of new flavors.)

5. The slow food movement: slowing down to eat lowers stress and lengthens lifespan. Cheese can help make that happen; it is a food that is easy to savor and pleasurable to eat.

---

6. Cheese is tasty! (Who doesn't like cheese? What's wrong with them?)

7. It has fun names that make you laugh (Havarti, Munster, and Manchego).

---

[5] My friend and ever-diligent copyeditor, Marlowe Shaeffer, insisted I inform you that a zillion is not a real number. In fact, according to *http://cheese.com*, there are currently 670 different kinds.

8.  To learn about cheese is to learn about food.

9.  Macaroni and cheese. Why is it so popular in the U.S.? Was it popular before Kraft?

10. Can people get good cheese mail-order? Are there Internet resources on why to love cheese and how to get it?

With this simple outline, good things will happen. It's a foundation of ideas that supports whatever else you do. It is now impossible to eat the microphone. Whatever slides you make, images you use, or movies you show, there is always a simple, clear structure for what you're doing and why. As your talk develops, the outline might change, but you will still have clear points to offer. So, if during your presentation you get lost, your laptop explodes, or your notes become incomprehensible, fall back on the outline. You can still give some amount of value just by running through the outline and making your points.

Some people resist outlines because in our modern age they seem rigid, low-tech, and old-school, restricting ideas to the tyranny of two-dimensional hierarchy. They think it's cooler to use less constrained forms of organization like mindmaps or storyboards. Good books like Garr Reynolds's *Presentation Zen* (New Riders) and Nancy Duarte's *Slide:ology* (O'Reilly) advocate such things. Try different ones to figure out which creative process works best for you.

But there must be an outline of points supporting whatever you put into your talk for this reason: all presentations are narratives, and all narratives are a sequence of points. Even if your points are made by images, stories, or puppet shows, they must be linked together in a narrative to provide value to the audience. And that narrative must reflect the promise offered by the title. An outline like the previous example is the simplest narrative structure to work from. It's easy to remember. You can even use that outline in your slides, showing your audience your plan as you go.[6] And even if you spend 20 hours building an amazing slide deck, but someone in the front row runs off with your laptop right after slide #2, you can fall back on the outline. It won't be great, but you'll be OK. It's much harder to fall back on a storyboard,

---

[6] The downside to revealing everything is that you lose the element of surprise, which is useful in making narratives interesting. But what you gain in clarity and confidence is probably worth the trade.

a mindmap, or just about anything else, unless you've used those approaches to arrive at something like a simple outline.

I usually present with slides. I love using images and movies to make points, but I never worry that these things won't work. Having thought clearly through my points, even if I lose the specific way I had hoped to present them, I can still offer them to my audience. If I'm fluent in my research, I can offer those anecdotes naturally. In effect, by working hard on a clear, strong, well-reasoned outline, I've already built three versions of the talk: an elevator pitch (the title), a five-minute version (saying each point and a brief summary), and the full version (with slides, movies, and whatever else strengthens each point).

It's no surprise that speakers who work without slides use simple outlines or short lists to keep to their points. Mark Twain, Winston Churchill, and Franklin Roosevelt all used a short outline of five or six points—often with just a few words per point—to help them recall their hour-long speeches while giving them. If you do enough thinking in advance, all your brain needs is a little list, and most of the speaking will take care of itself (see Figure 5-1).

*Figure 5-1. This is not a police photo. When I speak without slides, as I did here for Ignite! Seattle in 2006, I often use one folded Post-it note, listing my five points.*

It may turn out that if you pick a good title and it's on turf you know very well, then like Lincoln, you won't have to work very hard to fulfill the promise the title makes to your audience. And of course, if you are like Lincoln, you don't necessarily need an interesting title to do a great job. The Gettysburg Address is called the Gettysburg Address because Lincoln didn't bother to name it (some historian probably figured, "Well, he was at Gettysburg, and he addressed the audience, so..."). But remember, he was the president of the United States and could get a crowd whenever he wanted one. Unless you're famous enough to expect people to come because of your name or distinctive hatware, get to work. The more effort you put into the clarity of your points, the easier everything else about public speaking becomes.

# Photos you don't expect to see

Many interesting things happen in the corners, away from the spotlights. But most pictures of public speaking focus on center stage. Over the next few pages, you'll find photos and stories of things I think you'd like to know.

This photo, taken in a Starbucks, reflects what it's like to travel to a speaking engagement and be stuck in uninteresting places along the way. Similar to being in a rock band on tour, there is little romance in getting from place to place. Even when the gig is somewhere amazing like Moscow or Tokyo, much time is spent waiting in the boring places you must go through to get to the interesting ones. Traveling alone has few upsides, and waiting alone at an empty airport is not one of them.

This moment was at the Vancouver International Airport at 6:30 a.m. while waiting to catch a 7:30 a.m. flight home. Only Starbucks was open that early. With nothing else going on, I tried to get some work done. If you look carefully, you'll see I've achieved several spectacularly useless doodles.

Travel, however, is excellent for finding new questions to ask, so I write often while on trips. My technology of choice is Moleskine notebooks, as shown in the picture above. I never leave home without one, and there are stacks of journals filled with ideas near my desk at home. I flip through them when I think I have nothing left to say.

Getting set up is more stressful than the talk itself. Only rarely are the lecterns as well stocked as this one on Microsoft's main campus, which has light controls, a lapel mike, and two microphones for the audience. In the bottom-left corner of the lectern is a case with pens, Post-it notes, and other handy things speakers often discover they need at the last minute.

Some AV staff are first rate pros, and run their rooms as if they were Carnegie Hall, making sure all the sound and video gear are fine tuned so I can do well. But some are not, and as I'm in many venues, I have little time to sort out the good from the bad. My paranoia around getting set up explains why I prefer to use my own laptop. If my laptop explodes, I'm to blame, and I'd rather it be my fault than put myself at the mercy of a tech guy I just met, who may have been hired yesterday and have even less of a clue than I do.

For a few years, I ran architecture tours of NYC, which provided new public speaking challenges. Hecklers in your own audience are one thing, but overcoming the distractions created by taxis, buses, vagrants, and confused tourists (who think you might be their tour guide) helped make ordinary speaking venues much easier to handle.

In Times Square, as shown in the picture above, if you can keep people's attention for more than 30 seconds—without slides and a microphone—you're doing well. If you count the number of people listening versus those who appear distracted, I was doing pretty well in this photo. That's me in the center.

Even when I'm on my game and things are going well, some people will always be doing something other than listening. Can't blame them, it's just how people are.

Look at how small I am in this guy's field of vision. It's very hard for me to compete with the computer screen right in front of his face or the cute girl in the next row. For this reason, sit in the cheap seats before your talk to remind yourself of how much energy you need to project so that you don't look like a zombie on stage.

In 2007 I got an email from a woman who found some typos in an essay on my website. As thanks, I offered to send her a copy of one of my books. She declined, saying she lived in Australia, which is quite far away. But ha! I told her I was going to be in her fine country giving a lecture the next month and could hand-deliver one. As it turned out, she was going to the very conference I was speaking at. The problem was, she was shy and would be hard to find. I told her not to worry—I have my ways.

My solution? I told this story to the audience at the start of my keynote lecture, who responded with an encouraging round of applause. Smiling, she came up to the stage so I could give her the book.

Being invited all over the world means I'm often treated as a special guest. Sometimes I meet famous and interesting people, and often there are after-parties and special dinners where I'm the guest of honor. However, frequently my nightlife looks something like the above, without the view.

But on this day in Chicago, the travel gods smiled upon me. After an upgrade to suite 614 at the Hotel Monaco and a fine lecture at DePaul University, I hid from the cold, rainy February night with an excellent meal and wine with a friend named Fitz. Riding the buzz of a travel experience done right in a favorite city, I wrote a good part of Chapter 3 while sitting in the window of my room, as shown above. For entertainment, I watched as cops, at 1:15 a.m., arrested a drunken shoplifter at the 7-Eleven across the street, where I'd bought snacks hours earlier.

When you strip away all of the layers, like slides and handouts, public speaking becomes intimate and real. It's just a person with ideas. This is how it's been done for thousands of years. There are good reasons few comedians use slides or props—those things can get in the way of connecting with the audience. This explains why I love short speaking formats like Pecha Kucha and Ignite! where the rules are different: five or six minutes per talk, and slides that move automatically or no slides at all. It forces speakers to take risks and be vulnerable, which always makes things more interesting for the audience. And it makes them cut most of the bullshit out of their presentations.

The photo above was taken at Gnomedex '08 in Seattle, Washington, during its afternoon Ignite! session. I didn't do very well that day, but the experience of doing unusual formats or speaking on new topics always teaches me something I can use next time.

There's something unnerving about large, empty rooms. They look like graveyards. Since I never know how many people will show, the bigger the room, the bigger the stakes. When I arrive, the rooms are always empty. It's just me, the tech guys (they are always men), and, if I'm lucky, an organizer to help me settle in.

It's interesting how the view from the lectern can vary from room to room—sometimes there's almost 20 feet between where I am and where the audience begins. I took these photos to give you a sense of what I see when I'm up on stage.

These are the same six rooms from the previous photo, now shown with actual crowds. I told them if they stood up and looked really happy, I'd put their photos in the book. I kept my word.

Speaking venues from left to right, top to bottom: IAAP, Bellevue, Washington; Adaptive Path MX, San Francisco, California; Waterloo UX at RIM, Waterloo, Ontario; T4G @ Toronto Science Center, Toronto, Ontario; Microsoft Corporation, Redmond, Washington; Ignite! Seattle, King Kat Theater, Seattle, Washington.

## CHAPTER 6

# The science of not boring people

There is a moment at every movie, symphony, and lecture, right before the show starts, when the entire audience goes silent. All the conversations and rustlings stop, and everyone, at about the same time, falls into quiet anticipation for what is about to happen. This is called the hush over the crowd, but really it's the moment when the crowd itself first forms. The 200 unique people with different thoughts and ideas now become one single entity, joining together for the first time to give their unified attention to the front of the room. And the strange part is that the audience gives control over to the unknown. They have not seen the movie before. They haven't heard the lecture or seen the play. It's an act of respect and an act of hope—and it's amazing. There are only a few things in the world that can silence a room full of people, and the beginning of a performance is one of them.

I get chills when it happens even if, like last week, I'm just in the back row of a movie theater about to watch *Crank: High Voltage*, a hopelessly silly action film. Even there, right after the previews and before the opening credits start, the sensation of listening to a crowded room trying to be silent is bizarre and magical at the same time. On this day, however, I broke the silence. A peanut M&M escaped from the stash in my hand, crashing to the floor. The sound of each and every bounce, as it rolled down to the front row, echoed in the ears of annoyed strangers. My clumsy violations, as embarrassing as they were, demonstrated how silence is rare, special, and easy to break.

And when I'm the speaker, I know that special moment is the only time I will have the entire audience's full attention. Unless an alien spaceship crash-lands on stage midway through the talk, the silence before I begin is the most powerful moment I have. What defines how well I'll do starts with how I use the power of that moment. The balance rests on a bigger question: how will I keep people's attention after that moment is gone? There's an easy way to keep score: what percentage of the people in attendance is listening? 70%? 50%? 1%? Even if 70% of the room is listening, a pretty good score, how many of them understand what I'm saying? Who knows. But for those not paying attention, there's no chance they'll gain anything from my talk. For me to have value, I have to keep the attention of as many people as possible.

The science is clear. No one can keep the undivided attention of his audience. Not really. How much uninterrupted attention do you ever get from your friends or coworkers? Or better yet, how often do you give all of your attention to someone else? Nodding your head every so often, while your spouse rambles on about his day at work, doesn't count if you're thinking about what's on TV. It's rare today to have more than a few undivided minutes with most people in your life. Email, Twitter, and mobile phones have made it worse, but it's always been a problem. Our species has survived because of millions of years of hunting and working, using our muscles and brains in the active pursuit of things. Sitting and listening to someone drone on and on—which, unfortunately, so many lecturers do—is an attention disaster. Our genetic nature opposes the design of a basic, everyday lecture-room environment.

This is far from a surprise, considering that most people avoid lectures when they can. No one says regretfully on his deathbed, "If only I'd gone to more lectures!" We know that the best way to learn something is by doing it, and in a lecture, you never do much of anything except sit and stare (two things few of us need to practice). So, if we must go, we sit in the back, bringing fully charged electronic escapes, and we select the lecture with the greatest chance of being interesting or entertaining. Consider how minimally lectures have changed in the last 200 years compared to the exponential growth of everything else. If you used a time-travel machine to bring the crowd at Gettysburg into the seats at your next annual corporate meeting, the only question they'd have is why so few people wear hats.

The science of attention—a topic popularized by books like Malcolm Gladwell's *Blink* (Back Bay Books)—can also be thought of as the science of boredom, which is a surprisingly useful way to think about how a speaker tries to keep people interested. If you can stop boredom from happening, and stop doing things that bore people, you're well on your way to having an attentive crowd. Professor Donald A. Bligh, while doing research for his book *What's the Use of Lectures?* (Jossey-Bass), strapped up his students to heart rate monitors during various lectures and measured what happened over time. It's no surprise that their heart rates declined. They peak at the magic moment of attention right at the start, and, on average, decline steadily (see Figure 6-1). With this depressing fact, it's easy to understand why most lectures are slow one-way trips into sedation. Our bodies, sitting around doing little, go into rest mode—and where our bodies go, our minds will follow.

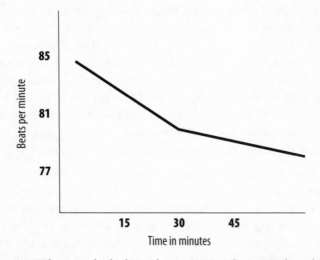

**Figure 6-1.** *What your body does when sitting at a lecture. Adapted from Donald A. Bligh's* What's the Use of Lectures? *(Jossey-Bass).*

John Medina, molecular biologist and director of the Brain Center at Seattle Pacific University, believes 10 minutes is the maximum amount of time most people can pay attention to most things. In his bestselling book *Brain Rules* (Pear Press), Medina spends an entire chapter applying this theory to the challenges of teaching— the 10-minute rule is at the core of how he plans his lectures. He never spends more than 10 minutes on a single point, and he makes sure to structure the entire lecture around a sequence of points he knows the audience is interested in hearing. With enough study about the audience's interests, and a 10-minute time limit, boredom can be kept at bay for an hour.

Ten is not a magic number, however. Lectures that are 8, 12, or even 45 minutes long can be captivating, provided the speaker knows what he's doing and understands how to keep people interested. But most don't. There is a good reason the most well-respected conference in modern times, the TED (Technology, Entertainment, Design) Conference, uses a mixture of 8- and 20-minute long talks at its events. At this ridiculously popular and supremely expensive lecture-centric event (tickets are $4,000 or more), famous minds like Bill Gates, Al Gore, Bono, and hundreds of other CEOs, political leaders, and geniuses in various fields, fly from all over the world to speak—but for a maximum of 20 minutes. They spend more time eating lunch than they do giving their presentations. This forces speakers to distill their message down to its most concise, passionate, potent form, so even if they fail to keep people's attention, they won't be on stage long enough to bore anyone to death.[1] Television sitcoms—a format that has been studied for decades to perfect its attention-capturing qualities—are also in the same time range: 30 minutes long, divided into thirds, and with generous helpings of 30-second commercials.

Most lectures are an hour long for no good reason other than we like that neat increment of time. If you have to hire a babysitter, drive to the venue, and find parking in a crowded lot, just to listen to someone speak for only 15 minutes, you'd be rightly upset. Either that, or you wouldn't bother going at all. Time is an easy way to measure value, which we can apply before we pay for whatever the thing happens to be. And for the host of the event, it's more convenient to schedule sessions for an hour or 90 minutes. It's challenging enough to wrangle one decent speaker (let alone managing his schedule and panic attacks); finding three or four additional speakers to fill each hour would only multiply the event planner's overhead. People often complain that they only learned a few things in an hour-long lecture, but would they be willing to go at all if the talk was only 10 minutes long?

Sadly, we'll always have long lectures for reasons that have nothing to do with the actual lectures at all. It's an artifact of culture, the logistics of putting together events, and the reluctance to change that ensures most people, until the end of time, will lecture longer than their audience can tolerate. And the cynical icing on this paragraph of frustrations is that even if you limit the average speaker to 20 minutes, or 10, there's no guarantee he'll use that time well. A true dullard can make any amount of time feel like too much.

---

[1] The amazing popularity of Pecha Kucha and O'Reilly's Ignite! events, which are comprised of presentations five or six minutes long, with automated slide decks, is fueled by the protection they provide from long, boring presentations. See *http://www.pecha-kucha.org/* and *http://ignite.oreilly.com/*.

But there's a solution. The answer to most attention problems is **POWER**.

Power is a fun word, even more so when you put it in bold and all caps for no reason. People get upset when you say you want more of it, but I'm going to claim every speaker should seek more power. I know in America we like to believe in democracy and the even distribution of power, but any political science major knows the United States, technically, is a republic. We distribute power unevenly by design; for example, we have 100 senators, 50 governors, and only one president, and each has magnitudes more power than the citizens he or she represents. Uneven distribution of power is necessary to get things done efficiently, which is exactly what you need when trying to give a lecture. If you think things are bad in America now, in a true democracy of 300 million people, they would be much worse.

The setup for public speaking is beyond republican—in the political science sense of the word—it's tyrannical. Only one person is on stage, only one person is given an introductory round of applause, and only one person gets the microphone. If the aliens landed during the TED Conference, they'd obviously assume the guy standing on stage holding the microphone was supreme overlord of the planet. For much of the history of civilization, the only public speakers were chiefs, kings, and pharaohs. But few speakers use the enormous potential of this power. Most speakers are so afraid to do anything out of the ordinary that they squander the very power the audience hopes they will use.

## Set the pace

The easiest way to use power is to set the pace. Everyone fantasizes about being the lead guitarist or singer of his favorite band, but the real power is in the rhythm section. It controls the speed at which everything happens—too fast, too slow, or hopefully just right. That task usually falls to the drummer, the guy who is always near the back of the stage (in part because he has the loudest instrument). At any time, he could bring things to a halt by stopping playing altogether or by slamming on the bass drum as fast as he can. In either case, that fancy guitar solo will end embarrassingly fast. Other than smashing the drummer on the head with his Stratocaster, the guitarist can never overpower the drummer's rhythm.

The drummer is really the person with the most power, just as the person with the microphone at a lecture is. A speaker must set the pace for the audience if he wants to keep their attention. Your average dive bar cover band can get a crowd moving simply because they set a clear pace. People love rhythm. We love to feel in sync. But the only person who can ever set that rhythm is the person with power at the front of the room.

I've spoken at universities and corporations to people far smarter than I am, who are funnier and more creative over lunch than I am all day, but I can still give them a good lecture by providing an easy-to-follow rhythm. I can say, "I have 30 minutes to talk to you, and five points to make. I will spend five minutes on each point and save the remaining time for any questions." That takes about 10 seconds to say, but for that small price I continue to own the attention of the room because they know the plan. They know the pace. If at any time they tune out—lost in dreams of sexy, friendly people on Hawaiian beaches—and suddenly snap back to reality, they should be able to think, "Wow, I totally spaced out. What is he talking about? Oh, OK, he's on point three of five. Got it." Even the most attentive audiences drift in and out of focus, and I have to make sure it's easy for them to rejoin my talk when their daydreams end.

Once you have everyone's attention, briefly outline how things will work. You'll automatically earn 10 bonus points. They won't even care much about the details of your plan, provided it's easy to follow and you don't spend much time explaining it. Something is wrong if 60 seconds go by and you aren't already into your first point. Don't waste time giving your resume or telling the back story ("I first read about blah blah at blah blah"). They don't care. They almost never need to know how you got where you are. If they chose to be in the audience after just reading the talk title, description, and your bio, they think you are plenty credible. Start with a beat. Think of your opening minute as a movie preview: fill it with drama, excitement, and highlights for why people should keep listening.

Rhythm creates energy. A steady, pulsing rhythm explains all forms of dance, from country line dancing to a 3 a.m. Ecstasy-fueled rave. Military marches depend entirely on rhythms from drums or chants of "Left, left, left right left." But most people have an awful sense of time when they are performing, including some dancers and musicians. Take away the drummer who provides that steady beat, and the pulsing energy charging the dancers and musicians will disappear. Speakers have no drummer on stage, no back-up band to keep pace. If you're not paying attention to rhythm, your audience will soon find rhythms of their own inside their minds.

Some speakers claim they'll spend 5 minutes on the first of five points, and then 30 minutes later they're still talking about the first point, unaware they've betrayed the rhythm they promised. Don't let this happen to your nice, friendly, loving audiences. Look out for them. Drummers practice with a metronome, a little box that keeps perfect time. Your work is much easier: you don't have to be precise, you just have to be in the ballpark. Practice your material in front of a clock until you get the timing down— you can't know how long each slide or point will take until you do it. Having a clock in the room helps, but often there's too much going on to make adjustments on the fly. Remember: if you're too lazy to practice, expect your audience to be too lazy to follow.

## Direct the attention ("What am I looking at and why?")

There are some things the human mind loves paying attention to, including the following:

- Things we like to eat
- Things that might eat us
- Problems we relate to
- People we empathize with
- Topics we care about
- Puzzles we want to solve
- Bright, shiny moving objects (see car advertisements)
- People we want to have sex with (see all advertisements)
- Things that explode (men)
- Things that are pretty (women)
- Things that are pretty and explode (men and women)

With this list in hand, an easy trick would be to stick one of these things into your talk every five or six minutes just to jolt people's attention back to you. This doesn't work. It's too obvious. Standing at the front of the room blasting a foghorn while you drop your pants every 60 seconds will certainly keep everyone's attention, right up until they rush the stage to pummel you. People know when they are being manipulated. Showing a movie clip, telling a joke, or putting up a pretty picture that has nothing to do with your topic will have little lasting effect. It doesn't mean anything. Only well-chosen pictures are worth a thousand words, and, even then, they can only be valuable if they're displayed long enough for the audience to comprehend their meaning. If you find natural ways to draw attention to things that illustrate your point, use them.

The simplest way to do this is by telling stories. Frankly, as soon as you open your mouth, you are telling a kind of story. All communication has a narrative: a beginning, a middle, and an end. The best way to direct attention is to talk about situations (another word for a story) that the audience cares about. Then they have two reasons to be interested: the situation and who it's happening to. It's one thing to say, "Here's line 5 of the new tax code." That's just a boring fact, floating in space, encouraging people to put their attention elsewhere. It's quite another to say, "80% of you in the audience confused line 5 with line 6 on your last tax return, which cost you $500. Here's how to not make that mistake." Even a topic as mind-numbingly dull as tax forms becomes interesting if the speaker cares both about the problem and the people affected by it. When an audience is curious about the story you're telling, they'll follow your lead almost anywhere. Good storytellers know this intuitively. As Annette Simmons wrote in *The Story Factor* (Perseus):

> *You can entice, inspire, cajole, stimulate, or fascinate but you cannot make anyone listen to anything. Embracing this fact up-front lets us focus on what we can do. We want to create curiosity. We want to catch and hold someone's attention.... Influence is a function of grabbing someone's attention, connecting to what they already feel is important, and linking that feeling to whatever you want them to see, do, or feel. It is easier if you let your story land first, and then draw the circle of meaning/connection around it using what you see and hear in the responses of your listeners.*

If you do choose to do something fancy like show pictures, charts, or movies—or interpretive dances, musical performances, flaming chainsaw juggling, or any other possible thing you could do on stage to get attention—consider the following: "Why is the audience watching this?" Bad answers include: you think it's cool, you want to show off your chainsaw skills, or, perhaps the greatest sin of all, you feel obligated to fill the assigned time slot. You have to do better than that. The best reason is that it fits the story you are telling. Know what the point is and what insight the audience will gain from what you are directing their attention to. Go well out of your way to pause midway through a movie clip to emphasize the key things they are supposed to see or understand. If you're not sure what the point is, or whether it applies to the audience, cut it out of your material. It's better to keep the attention of the room for 10 solid minutes and then open for questions than to stumble through an hour in a stupor of mediocrity.

## Play the part: you're the star

People always have expectations. If they go to a fancy restaurant, they expect outstanding service and perhaps a snooty maître d' they can make fun of. If they see an action movie, they expect explosions that defy the laws of physics and plots with cave-size holes. And if they give you an hour of their time to talk to them, they expect you to be confident in what you say and do. If you fumble with the remote for your laptop, get confused by your own slides, or apologize for not being more prepared for the presentation, you are making it clear that you are not worthy of their attention. You are not playing the role they expect—that of a confident, clear, motivated, and possibly entertaining expert on something. You do not have to be perfect, but you do need to play the part.

In other words, be bigger than you are. Speak louder, take stronger positions, and behave more aggressively than you would in an ordinary conversation. These are the rules of performing. It's what kids in high school are taught when rehearsing for the annual production of "Annie Get Your Gun." They are the same rules that good stand-up comedians, professors, and talk-show hosts follow. Specific to lectures, consider this: if you are at the front of the room, how far away are the people in the middle rows?

Now realize half the audience is even farther away. Those people in the back need more help to connect with you and your message.

If you do webcasts, teleconferences, or otherwise speak through computers, this point is even more important. Being on a computer means you instantly fall from being three-dimensional to two. They can still see you, but it's a pixelated, washed-out, flat video version of you. The subtleties of your humor and the nuances of your points have a harder time coming through. To compensate, you have to project more energy. Doing so feels unnatural if you're sitting alone in your cubicle, but your onscreen audience needs every extra bit of energy they can get from you to keep their attention from sliding away.

A common mistake people make is to shrink onstage. They become overly polite and cautious. They speak softly, don't tell stories, and never smile. They become completely, devastatingly neutral. As safe as this seems, it is an attention graveyard. It's like being given the part of Hamlet—who has some of the best monologues in human history—and indifferently mumbling lifeless sentences into your sleeve. I'm not suggesting you should be phony. Don't act like a game-show host or a cheerleader. Instead, be a passionate, interested, fully present version of you.[2] That's who your audience came to hear.

## Know what happens next

The biggest advantage I have over every crowd, no matter how smart they are, is that I know what will happen next. I described this earlier in the book, but it deserves to be mentioned again because it's one powerful way to control attention. I'm convinced I could know half as much on a subject as my audience, yet still amaze, surprise, and entertain them by how I weave my stories together. This makes the transitions between slides critically important. I have to know what's coming next and set up what I say on the current slide to make the following pay off. If I know this, I can summon the room's attention at the right time to make

---

2  The study of acting is not the practice of being fake. It's learning how to become more expressive as yourself and applying that to life on stage and off. All communicators benefit from learning about theater. See *An Actor Prepares*, Constantin Stanislavski (Theatre Arts Book).

sure they are all looking at or listening to me when the next thing I'm going to say is funny, important, or powerful.

Doing this well depends on how much I practice. I can't remember the transitions between points or how one story will best tie in to the next unless I've rehearsed and learned how to do it. Often I throw away a great idea because I can't figure out how to get smoothly into it from the previous story, or get from that great idea into the next story. Also, invest in software like PowerPoint or Keynote, which have presenter modes that allow you to see the next slide on your laptop only. This tool will help prepare you to make a smooth transition, just like you practiced.

## Tension and release

If I tell you someone will win a million dollars before this paragraph is over, I have introduced drama. Who will win? Why will they win it? Suddenly, reading paragraphs is thrilling. Drama is one easy way to build tension. All great experiences involve a dramatic rhythm of tension and release, whether it's a masterful magic show, a rollercoaster ride, or a flirtatious first date on a blanket by the sea at sunset. And in all cases, tension is created by the suggestion of releasing it. If I said someone *might* win a million dollars, or there is a slim chance you *might* get laid, it's not as interesting. There must be a reasonable expectation that the payoff will happen.[3] If you're smart, that payoff is made clearly in the title and description of your presentation.

The simplest kind of tension to build and then release is the one I mentioned before: problem and solution. If your talk consists of several problems important to the audience, and you promise to release the tension created by those problems by solving each one, you'll score big. The audience will follow you through each sequence of tension and release. If you do a great job with the first problem you identify, and offer a practical or inspiring way to handle it, they'll stay with you throughout your entire talk. Other kinds of tension can be created by the premise of the talk. Your subject could be, "Why no one should go to school." Your entire

---

3  Anton Chekhov once wrote, "One must not put a loaded rifle on the stage if no one is thinking of firing it." Good storytellers put guns in their stories and know how and when to fire them (and who to fire them at).

line of thinking creates a kind of tension, which you will release with each fact offered and point made.

Patterns of tension and release can simultaneously be used to establish a rhythm. The top-10 list, popularized on David Letterman's late-night talk show, is one system for both generating an easy rhythm and creating various levels of tension and release. As the list is read and descends closer to #1, the audience's anticipation is building the whole time as to what the top answer will be.

## Get the audience involved

At the beginning of my public-speaking career, I never involved the audience simply because I was terrified of them. I found that when I let people ask me questions midway through the talk, I'd get flustered and never regain my initial confidence level. So, I did the only sensible thing I could think of: tell people at the beginning not to ask any questions until the end. This was a bad solution, attention-wise; they'd become immediately disinterested upon hearing that the next hour was going to be an uninterrupted lecture (I'd often go for 80 minutes, earning my own private corner of attention hell). Every audience has plenty of energy that, when channeled, even if only in small amounts, always invigorates their attention levels. Eventually, I learned some easy tricks for getting an audience involved without spoiling my rhythm:

- **Ask for a show of hands.** Not sure how experienced your audience is? Ask them, "Who here has been in their current profession for less than five years?" Suddenly, you'll know much more about the crowd. They can't gauge the response, so make sure to describe what you see: "OK, looks like about 70% of you. Great." During your talk, you can also use the audience to get feedback about your pace. Ask, "How many of you think I'm going too slow?", followed by, "How many think I'm going too fast?" You now have real-time data and can adjust accordingly.

- **Ask trivia and let people shout out answers.** The stupidest thing for a speaker to ask his audience is, "Any questions on what I just said?" This sounds threatening, like he's daring you to challenge his authority, which many people won't want to take on. Instead, make it positive and interactive. Say, "Is there anything you'd like me to clarify?" During your talk, let the audience help tell your stories or show what they know: "Anyone here know who invented cheesecake?" Then give out prizes, decent things like copies of your book, items you know are popular with the crowd, or $10 gift certificates to Starbucks. The audience attention level will definitely rise.

- **Give them a problem to solve.** If you know of interesting, challenging problems related to your topic, pose them to your audience. Pick problems small enough that they can be solved in 30–60 seconds. For a lecture on travel smarts, ask, "What would you do if someone stole your wallet while you were on vacation?" Or, in a talk about cooking, "How would you recover from burning all the steaks for your six dinner guests due to arrive in 20 minutes?" Be specific, be dramatic, and choose questions that have clear, direct answers, and you'll get responses from the room. Ask them to work with their neighbors or in small groups. Always give slightly less time than they need to add some fun pressure.

Every audience is different, so interaction can be risky. When you allow someone in the audience to speak, you are giving him the floor and with it some of your power. The good news is, he'll nearly always give the power back to you. Sometimes, he'll give you even more power in the form of his attention and positive energy. And even if no one answers the questions you're asking, more people will be listening to the silence in the room than were listening to you talking before the room went silent. You have, regardless of why, regained the audience's attention.

## You are judge, jury, and executioner

If you ask people not to use cell phones, and someone answers a call in the front row, what should you do? It's up to you to enforce the house rules because you have the microphone. Or what about the guy who asks a question that goes on for three whole minutes? How long will you let him ramble on? Twenty seconds is more than enough time for a question; after 40 seconds, it's a monologue and everyone in the audience hates him. But after a minute, people will be staring at you. You are allowing all of the energy to be sucked out of the room. They can't do much about it, but they know you can.

Never be afraid to enforce the rules you know the room wants you to follow. When in doubt, ask the room for a show of hands: "Should we continue with this topic or move on?" If they vote to move on, that's what you should do. When you enforce a popular rule, you reengage everyone who supports that rule. You restore your power and earn the audience's respect. So, don't hesitate to cut off a blowhard, silence the guy on his cell phone, and interrupt the table having a private but distracting conversation. As long as you are polite and direct, you'll be a hero.

## Always end early

People want to leave early, but when those same people get the microphone, they run late. Don't be like them. Always plan and practice to end early. If a window of opportunity presents itself to finish a few minutes ahead of schedule—giving your audience a head start on beating traffic, getting to their next meeting, or attacking the snacks in the conference hall—do it. No one ever wants you to go longer. If people really love you, they'll often stick around to hear more of what you have to say. Let everyone else escape. Give the audience your email address, and stress that you'll happily answer additional questions over email. Be as generous and giving of your time as you like, but make sure people are opting in, not being forced to listen to you more. Be an attention liberator and set them free. Case in point: this chapter is over.

## CHAPTER 7

# Lessons from my
# 15 minutes of fame

It's May of 2008, and I'm at CNBC studios dressed in black shoes, black pants, and a black turtleneck, staring into a camera surrounded by bright white lights. Looking into a wall of lights seems like heaven until you realize that you can't see anything, your eyes hurt, and it's fucking hot. With each passing second, it's less clear whether the goal is to film me or to see how long it takes for me to melt like the witch from *The Wizard of Oz*. Perhaps it's both. On the ground is a strip of masking tape that marks where my feet need to stay as the 10-person film crew surrounds me with various gear, cameras, light filters, and microphones, ensuring I look fantastic as I embarrass myself on national television. Despite how hard it is to stand still for so long, the real challenge is that I'm expected to do the worst kind of nothing—the kind of nothing where I have no distractions while everyone stares, prods, and pokes me—as I wait and wait for them to be ready for me to say my lines. To stop my mind from exploding due to the sheer helplessness of being trapped in permanent hurry-up-and-wait mode, I focus on the drama playing out every few minutes behind the crew, drama only I can see.

It goes like this: CNBC employees come into the café to get a bite to eat but stop mid-stride, surprised at the site of me in their fancy cafeteria, clad in all black, illuminated by a sea of lights like the leader of the scary aliens in a sci-fi movie. Saddened by the discovery that their lunchroom has been converted into an enormous glowing soundstage, they glare at me for a long moment before turning back to the halls to search for other provisions. They glare with the same disdain you'd have for the asshole who smiles as he steals your parking space. I want to tell them it's not my fault. I want to point at the crew so they share the blame, but there is no escape. I am clearly the target of their hate for the rest of the afternoon. Standing alone on the set, an entire crew orbiting around me, it must appear as though I think I'm the center of the universe, a concept which—given the many layers of embarrassment running through my mind—could not be further from the truth.

I'm at CNBC to film a five-hour primetime TV series called *The Business of Innovation* (Figure 7-1). It's a media jackpot for an independent like me, so I'm trying as hard as possible not to screw it up. But in these moments on the first day of taping, dressed like a Steve Jobs impersonator (at CNBC's request), I'm feeling 10% adrenalin, 20% fear of embarrassment, and 70% complete and utter panic.

There are too many contradictions for me to hold on to sanity. First, I have no idea what is going on, yet I'm the center of attention, much like how it would feel to be invited over for dinner by a family of cannibals. Second, I'm a star of the show, yet I have no control and no shortage of people telling me what to do. Third, I'm fascinated by everything and want to ask hundreds of questions but can't because I'm surrounded by busy film professionals who have little patience for my curiosity. Even if I were a narcissist, even if I loved seeing myself on film (which I don't), it would be impossible not to panic and think I've made a big and permanent mistake—after all, bloopers last forever on YouTube. If they post any of my flubs online, including the take where my fly was open, it will be more famous than anything else I ever do.

*Figure 7-1. The B-roll footage for The Business of Innovation. Notice the chair in the background, a chair no one ever sat in.*

The good news for me is that I'm only one of five experts for the series, and I know I can hide behind the others at any time. We make quite a crew: Vijay Vaitheeswaran writes for the *Economist*, Keith Yamashita runs his own innovation consulting firm, Ranjay Gulati teaches at Harvard University, and Suzy Welch writes for *Business Week*. Headlining the show is Maria Bartiromo, the star anchor for CNBC (even cooler, she's the only woman in history to have a tribute song written to her by Joey Ramone). And on top of this, each hour-long episode is packed with a rock-star list of

CEOs, politicians, luminaries, and venture capitalists, including Jack Welch (former CEO of GE), Howard Schultz (CEO of Starbucks), Marc Ecko (fashion mogul), and Muhammad Yunis (Nobel Peace Prize recipient in 2006). The impressive lineup continues with the CEOs of Zappos, Kodak, LG, Xerox, FedEx, and Sirius Radio, as well as executives from Harley-Davidson, Timberland, Procter & Gamble, and on it goes. But for all the massive power of these featured guests, you'd be most surprised by one thing: they were just as afraid of being on television as I was.

Despite their entourages, fame, and ridiculous levels of success and media exposure, nearly everyone seemed just as disoriented by television as I was. No one talked about this, of course. It's like being bored at a funeral—most are, but no one wants to admit it first. But I saw their jittery hands, heard their nervous questions, and sat in many long, awkward, tense silences with these very famous people. There was regular caffeine and sugar abuse, and the green room[1] was packed with an arsenal of such provisions. The producers know that many people shut down from nerves and shrink to whispers when on camera, as some of these executives did on the show. So, the producers err on the side of a caffeine-and-sugar-induced fistfight with a co-host than sedate mumbles and soft shrugs.

To assuage their fears, many high-powered executives travel with staff, media experts, or heads of PR. These folks follow their clients around on the set, mediating discussions, approving decisions, and whispering private advice to them. It doesn't seem to help; in fact, the people who bring PR staff with them are the ones who probably have more to be worried about. Herb Kelleher (founder of Southwest Airlines) and Jack Welch were all on their own, and the friendliest and funniest people I talked with on the show.

The real killer in all this, the thing no PR or flunky can compensate for, is the waiting. Many people can work themselves into the right mindset to do fine on television, but there is so much hurrying up to wait that it's hard to time the mindset with the opportunity to use it. You get ready, you get psyched, and then uh oh,

---

[1] No one knows why they're called *green rooms*, and none of the ones I've been in were green. They usually feel like a dentist's waiting room, filled with nervous people who don't want to be there. The only plus is that there's food.

another reason to wait 10 minutes. It's shocking for CEOs and luminaries to learn their time is not as valuable to the network as it is to their companies. They will be forced to arrive early, wait around, and wait some more as needed to serve the making of the show.

What few understand is that the world of TV has its own place in the space–time continuum—every second matters more to them than to the rest of the working world. Despite the power of the Web, it's TV that still has the most money at stake per second of product. Case in point: based on my bestseller *The Myths of Innovation*, CNBC flew me across the country to interview me to appear as an expert on the show. The interview lasted exactly 33 minutes. So for 10 hours of flight and travel time for me to get to NYC, I spent less than an hour interviewing to appear on a TV show. They covered my costs and hotel, as they would throughout filming, but it was always clear: I was working for them, not the other way around. For the true star guests of the show, those with entourages or their own private islands, it must have been baffling to rearrange their busy executive travel schedules, fly across the country, drive all afternoon in traffic to get to CNBC, and wait for hours in a studio just to be filmed for exactly 4 minutes and 30 seconds (of which, perhaps half is used on air in the final edit). It was likely the most humbling experience they had all year. They shared the same look of disbelief when, on set, they were told, "That's a wrap, great job!", just when they felt they were getting warmed up. They expected to have the same star power as in the rest of their lives, forgetting to realize that in the world of TV, they are just another cog in the machine.

Speaking of making the show, the wall of lights I'm standing in front of in Figure 7-1 is for taping what's called *B-roll*. When I ask what the B-roll is, I'm told it's everything that's not the A-roll. Asking a rookie question gets you a sardonic answer; sarcasm and jargon reign in the stressful world of television. TV people seem bright and upbeat but also high-strung and impatient. Nothing happens fast enough for them. I'd later learn that the *A-roll* is the primary footage for the show, whereas the B-roll is the intros, credits, and other secondary footage. When you are watching TV, B-roll is what appears during the credits or between commercials, the bits of footage you never think about. It's easy to forget that someone produces every single second of television. When you see Dr. House (from his eponymous show) on TV, even if just for a commercial advertising the program, it means a crew spent hours setting up the lights. If you hear him speak, it means sound engineers spent hours setting up microphones and mixing sound. There is an expensive back story to every split-second of broadcast media, as every choice costs money and is done for specific reasons. And if they do it right, you never even think about it.

Have you ever been in a bar as brightly lit as the one on *Cheers*? Or a hospital as cheery as on *Scrubs*? We know television isn't real, but if done right, the consistent lack of reality creates its own immersive world. They call this *suspension of disbelief*. Even for nonfiction shows like *The Business of Innovation* or *The Daily Show with Jon Stewart*, what you see is never actually what happened during taping. There is editing. There is sound mixing. Camera lenses change how people look. There are hundreds of deliberate choices made for specific reasons, which explains why the B-roll is filmed in the cafeteria and not the studio. They want it to look very different from the A-roll, and with $200,000 worth of lights, gear, backdrops, and effects, the cafeteria looks instead like a conference room on the *Starship Enterprise*. You'd never guess where we shot it if I hadn't told you, even if you worked at CNBC. The viewers will never know how silly it felt to stand there in the cafeteria, how many takes it took for me to get each line right, or how ridiculous the whole thing was during filming. And even watching the B-roll myself, it was hard to connect what I experienced with what was actually televised.

## We perform all the time

The big lesson from being on television is simple: we are always performing. Any time you open your mouth and expect someone to listen, you are behaving differently than you would if you were alone. Admitting this doesn't make you a phony—it makes you honest. We are social creatures and behave differently to fit into different social situations. Here's an example. Think of a funny story or joke you know well.[2] Now imagine telling that joke three different times:

---

[2] In a pinch you can use this one: "How many Zen masters does it take to screw in a light bulb? Answer: None. The Zen master has overcome his desire for the bulb to be changed." Or, if your humor runs lower brow: "What do you call an Italian hooker? Answer: A pastatute."

1. To your best friend on your couch

2. To five friends over dinner at a restaurant

3. To 20 of your coworkers in a boardroom

In each case you are performing to achieve an effect, primarily to make your audience laugh. Each situation might be different, so the way you tell the joke will change. The same is true every time you open your mouth to speak. You always have a goal, whether it's to express a thought, ask a question, or make an observation. In trying to achieve that goal you are, in a sense, performing. And the bigger the audience, the bigger you need to be. Your voice needs to be louder, your hand gestures more dramatic, and your pace more upbeat. This is especially true for television. Since your appearance might be on a tiny TV in someone's living room or in a browser window on his computer, you have to act big to project yourself across that distance.

Having done most forms of public speaking, I've learned that television, radio interviews, YouTube videos, high school theater, podcasts, and monologues are simply different kinds of performances. Some are more intense than others, like being on national television, or require more practice and rehearsal, like acting in a stage play, but the basic rules are the same. Most people say they're afraid of performing for an audience, but this is bullshit. Unless you are living alone on a private island and have your groceries mailed to you, you have an audience every time you open your mouth. If you can talk to your mom on the phone for an hour or have an all-night fight with your boyfriend, you know most of what you need to communicate. And you already know how to perform. You know how to express anger, fear, passion, joy, and confusion. You know how to be dramatic, how to attract attention, and most importantly, how to convert what you're thinking into words that you say and actions you do. It's just a question of doing it at the right level for the environment you're in.[3]

---

3  One trick is to study what the user experience is like for people on the other end of whatever medium you're in. For example, if you're presenting via video conference, make sure you've sat in as an observer on someone else's. Then you'll have a sense for how you'll appear when it's your turn. At the taping of episode 2, they showed us some of episode 1, and it was immensely helpful in calibrating my behavior.

Oprah, Conan O'Brien, and Katie Couric know how to talk to the camera as if they were talking to a friend. It's their ability to make the strange, awkward world of broadcast seem normal—even comfortable—that explains why viewers like watching them. Howard Stern talks to his audience as if he were having beers with his buddies, which is why people tend to love him or hate him. Success often stems from the ability to make whatever medium you're in feel like something simpler and often less formal. It's the art of making the unnatural seem natural.

Few people think of television or radio as public speaking, which is strange when you run the numbers. By definition, being broadcast means that you will be seen by way more people than anything you normally do. The first time I was on TV was in 1997 on a small cable show, *CNET TV*; my appearance lasted a total of 180 seconds. It was entirely miserable, embarrassing, and paralyzing. I had no coaching and only limited media exposure. Whatever that experience was, it certainly did not feel like speaking, as I mostly mumbled and tried to get my hands to stop shaking. I remember how weird it felt to wear makeup (everyone on TV wears makeup), and how absurd it was to have a half-dozen bright lights aimed right at my face. I remember thinking: how do they expect me to see, much less say anything?

Being on television or radio, where millions of people will get to see and/or hear you, requires speaking in a studio devoid of an audience. Instead of a crowd of people, there is a circle of lights and producers. Instead of interested, friendly faces, there are cold, lifeless cameras and large, shiny microphones. When you watch the nightly news, you see Brian Williams or Katie Couric behind a nice desk, on an interesting-looking stage with a smart background. It's all sharp, classy, new, and put together with care. But anything not visible on camera, which is the majority of the room Katie or Brian sits in, probably looks like the engine room of a Navy battleship.

There are tall black walls, exposed ductwork, electronics, and gear everywhere. The fancy graphics you see over their shoulders or the tickers scrolling across the bottom of your TV do not exist anywhere in the studio. In their place is empty space reserved for those digital additions. On the studio floor in front of Katie, or in my case, Maria Bartiromo, engineers scurry about in headsets and talk in whispers. There are places where you're warned not to step, and long stretches of time when you cannot make a sound. There are no windows. There are no plants. There is nothing comfortable or friendly about it. Simply put, a TV studio is an expensive machine for making TV shows. Everything works in service of the mythical audience, but that audience is not present. TV studios are flat-out unpleasant, unfriendly environments, more like factory floors or scientific laboratories than comfy, supportive, warm places. Even though all the producers and production assistants were fun, smart, and attentive, they can't overcome the relentless pace of the process. The set at CNBC for *The Business of Innovation* had the additional challenge of being mostly virtual, except for the platform and couch. We shot against a blue screen with the entire set filled in digitally later (see the before and after in Figures 7-2 and 7-3). Does that couch look comfortable to you?

*Figure 7-2. The set at CNBC for* The Business of Innovation.

It's true that many stages and auditoriums aren't friendly either, but by contrast to a TV studio, I can always see or hear what's going on—who's listening, who's bored. My senses work to my advantage. And if I happen to say something completely stupid and inappropriate, like perhaps forget where I am and claim how great it is to be in Boston when I'm actually lecturing somewhere in NYC, I know instantly how the crowd feels about what I said,

*Figure 7-3. The set as seen on broadcast. That's me in the middle in the white shirt.*

even if it's only their desire to kill me. I always have the chance to respond to how the audience is responding to me. But there is no audience feedback in most TV studios. This means you might say exactly what the audience hoped, perhaps the secrets to instant weight loss or how to achieve immediate world domination (or peace, if you're a sissy), but you would get no real-time reaction. Alternatively, it means you can lie, talk too much, talk too little, be an idiot, or be brilliant, and have very little sense of what it is you are actually being.

The lesson I learned from this is that any time you are videotaped or recorded live without an audience, whether it's for TV or the Web, it's far worse being in an empty room than a tough room. This is why some shows have live audiences. They want to give their guests the many advantages of having the support and energy of real people. But most TV studios don't have audiences. So, if you've ever wondered why people on TV seem phony, stiff, irritable, or unnatural, it's in part because there's no natural feedback loop for their behavior. On many news shows, the only company is in the form of talking heads on satellite, people in similarly isolated environments thousands of miles away.

Once when I was on MSNBC via satellite from Seattle, I had my first chance to be a talking head. Whenever you see someone interviewed on the news and put in a little virtual box on the screen, in reality they're talking from inside a small studio near wherever they happen to be (Figure 7-4). To help viewers sort this out, they put a cardboard poster with the skyline of wherever they are up behind them to help clue you in. You never get to see what these studios look like, in part, because they're not interesting (thus the cardboard backdrop). Speaking from within one is worse than the challenges of the main studio since I can't even see the people I'm supposed to be speaking to. You're just stuck in a small room that's as charming as a large janitor's closet, with a camera pointed at your face.[4] Unless the show I'm on pays a few extra bucks for a live feed, I can't even see the video of what's being taped. All I get is an earpiece where a producer I've never met and can't see mostly tells me to wait, while I stare blankly into the lights. I've learned there's a special kind of anxiety when you're waiting alone in a room but know that at any moment you'll be broadcast across the country.

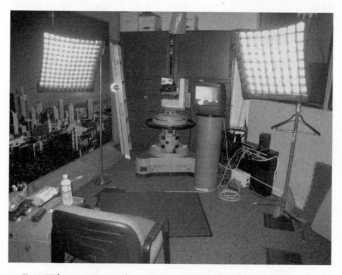

*Figure 7-4. What you see when you're a talking head.*

---

4 Often the people who run these studios are warm and friendly, as was the case at Fisher Pathways studios in Seattle where the picture was taken. They answered my many questions and did their best to prepare me, but they have better things to do than babysit guests for remote TV shows.

The secret to speaking to an audience without one actually present is to forget the studio and ignore the cameras (Figure 7-5). Go to a place in your mind where you remember the last time you spoke to a live, friendly, interested group, and match that style of behavior and enthusiasm. Speak as if that same audience is listening, and you'll be fine. Great hosts help you do this by feeding you energy and support, or even a softball question or two. All performers have a mindset they use when everything else is going wrong, and that's what gets them through. Much like in public speaking, I learned from my experience filming at CNBC that I just had to switch off the worried part of my brain and laugh at how bizarre it all was. I bought the ticket by coming on the show—I should get as much as I can from taking the ride.

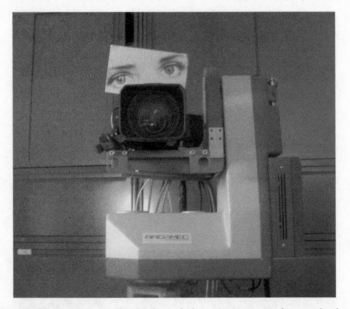

*Figure 7-5. As creepy as this looks, it helps. Having something to look at other than the Terminator-like glare of the camera lens is a good trick to help you seem more comfortable.*

Over the month it took flying back and forth from Seattle to NYC to tape the episodes (five times in all), I overcame most of the challenges of being on television. I had a great time. I mean, how could I not? I felt entirely like Charlie in *Charlie and the Chocolate Factory*, except my golden ticket showed me how TV, not candy, is made.

I met amazing people well out of my league, and interviewed and debated them as equals. But most of all, being involved for five episodes gave me the rare opportunity to improve with each hour-long episode, something few people are on TV enough to ever get to do. These days, I'm confident I can go with the flow no matter what happens—on TV or off.

Early on, I realized the prospect of being on national TV, on a show other than *America's Most Wanted* or *Jerry Springer*, was an honor of sorts, even if I were to screw up in some way. Most people never even get the chance to make mistakes that visible. And right before every taping I'd remember the last time I watched TV: flipping through channels, zipping through different shows, having a few beers, and mostly zoning out. I reminded myself no matter how many millions of people might end up watching, most of them won't be very interested in how smart or stupid I sound. I'm just one of hundreds of other people on TV at the same time. What seem like catastrophic embarrassments to me will be instantly forgotten, or possibly not even noticed, by others. And if what I say bores people, they'll change the channel. So what? Life goes on, and most of the world won't ever care.

## Teleprompters (and memorization) are evil

There was one obstacle I never overcame. I've met my public speaking nemesis, and it's not hecklers or tough rooms. It's the teleprompter. Until I was on *The Business of Innovation*, I'd never actually seen a teleprompter. I'd heard of them. I vaguely understood what they did. But the big surprise is that they are integrated into the cameras. When you look into the lens, which you are directed to do for things like B-roll, you see whatever words you're supposed to say, scrolling upward like the intro to *Star Wars*. In this case, my lines were short promotional sentences for the show. Goofy things like, "Innovation will transform the future" or "Breakthroughs are more important than they ever were." Vague, fluffy comments that mean nothing if you think about them for more than five seconds. It's the kind of thing I make fun of other people for saying or writing in their books. The producers on the show did let us edit copy for the actual lead-ins, but on day one there was no time, so we read what they had prepared.

I figured I'd ad lib around these bits of dialog, confident I could provide the effects the producers wanted (pithy and provocative was the goal), but with language that wasn't so annoying. No problem. I'm good at improvisation…or so I thought.

When I stood all in black in the CNBC cafeteria on that first day, staring into the lights and the cameras, pressured to satisfy everyone around me (and to get off the set as quickly as possible), I looked into the camera…and totally choked. Instead of being creative and original, I actually just said the text in the tele- prompter. I didn't really want to—it sounded even stupider than I imagined. But I couldn't stop. During this B-roll filming session, I had the chance to say five different lines, one for each episode. And since they let me have multiple takes, toward the end, feeling more confident, I tried to say something other than what the tele- prompter commanded. I practiced it quickly in my mind to mem- orize it. I used my full powers of concentration and had my improvised version of the line down cold. And when the director shouted, "Action!", I looked into the camera and said, to my own surprise, exactly what was on the teleprompter. I may as well have been lobotomized. You could have put the entire contents of *Green Eggs and Ham* in that thing, and I'd have read every last word. Figure 7-6 shows my view on the set.

*Figure 7-6. On right is camera 2, with the teleprompter showing my lead- in. At left is the monitor of what camera 2 saw, which in this case is me taking this picture.*

Teleprompters are used by many TV shows, including news broadcasts. It's another reason I suspect many newscasters sound the same, speaking in that disembodied, distant, I-might-actually-be-a-robot voice. With a teleprompter in your face, it's hard to ad lib, it's hard to pause, and, most of all, it's hard to be natural. Perhaps if I wrote the copy myself or got to know the producers better, I'd feel differently about these things. But it was the one part of actually speaking on television that got in my way. I hope someday I'll get the chance to have another go at conquering these things. For now, whenever I watch television and stare into the eyes of people speaking into the camera, all I can think about are the words scrolling past, being read as if they were their own.

## CHAPTER 8

# The things people say

I'm in Sydney, Australia, in 2006, and I just gave what I think is a killer presentation. The audience laughed at my jokes and enjoyed my stories, and my points hit home. It could not have gone better, and I'm sky-high from the buzz. I hop off the stage and Cory, one of the organizers, tells me enthusiastically, "You were fantastic! Totally amazing!" I shrug it off as if I'm too cool to take a compliment. Basking in the warm glow of my own ego, I happily stand with Cory and watch the next speaker. Turns out, he's bad. He's dull and unclear, his points are a mess, and the audience looks ready to leave. I feel for Cory—I know how awkward it is to talk to speakers after they bomb. When the speaker finishes and exits the stage, he's greeted by Cory just as I was. I can't look, but I want to: it's like a car accident happening in slow motion. And then I hear Cory say, "You were fantastic! Totally amazing!" The verbatim praise he gave me. Given the laws of physics in this universe, it's impossible we earned the same score. Maybe I deserved an F and him an A, but no functioning brain could score us equally. In that moment, I learned that the things people say often mean something other than what you think they mean. In this case, "totally amazing" did not mean I was amazing at all. It was just a post-lecture encouragement Cory gave each speaker, regardless of his performance.[1] If I wanted data on how well I'd done, I would have to look elsewhere.

How do you know how good you are at what you do? Probably from your boss, or maybe your coworkers. But I don't have a boss—no performer does. It's easier to find out how popular you are, but that's not the same as being good. And since people have their own preferences, what's good for one person isn't good for another. Above all else, people are bad at giving feedback. We often focus on the superficial ("Did you see that shirt?") or have our own opinions swayed by how others feel. Now and then, someone complains if I swear a few times, even if it's appropriate and in the spirit of things. And feedback is subjective, meaning one person's, "You were awesome," equals another's, "It was mediocre." I had a boss who, when shown a design for something, would say, "Well, it's not horrible." For him, this was high praise.

---

[1] To be fair, the moment when someone leaves the stage is a bad time to say anything because it is likely that he's too distracted to hear what you say.

Had I shown him plans for the 2009 iPhone in 1995, he probably would have said, "This doesn't suck." He judged everything against an ideal so grand nothing could ever come close. Since I worked with him for years, I learned to calibrate what he said, teasing out the real meaning from his caustic comments (I'm sure you do this with certain people you know). But as a speaker, it's hard to calibrate. Feedback from the audience is a one-shot deal—either you can make sense of it or you can't.

Once after I finished a lecture at MIT, while standing among a circle of interested people asking questions, a student pushed his way forward. He shoved his laptop in my face, pointing with his free hand at all the things I'd said that he thought were wrong. Clearly, it was thrilling for him to give feedback; he was smiling, fully engaged, and passionate. Was it good that my lecture provoked such interest, or bad that he found so much he thought was wrong with what I'd said? The short answer: I believe any attention at all means you did something of value. But sorting out the value is not easy to do.

Writing books, giving lectures, or doing anything interesting puts you in a position to regularly hear conflicting feedback. One person says speak louder, another says softer. And sometimes the feedback isn't even about your work—you're just an easy target for whatever venom has been building up in their lives. You are simply the first thing people have been put in a position to judge after days of being cruelly judged by others. They want to vent, and vent all over you, especially if it's just on some feedback form where they can be anonymous.

But most often, people give mixed messages. I've had people tell me the workshop I taught was awesome and then ask a question I answered seven times already. I've ended lectures in complete silence, only to get the highest scores on surveys. And I've had big applause where almost no one wanted to talk to me after I was done. Feedback in life and in public speaking is bewildering. There is no panel of judges like in the Olympics, no scorecards or championship rings. You're on your own to sort out which bits of feedback matter, and more importantly, the differences between how you feel about how you did and how the audience seems to feel.

But before we sort this out, there's one important fact to know, illustrated best by the following situation.

Imagine you're at a lecture about the future of the human race by Professor Moxley, the department chair and overlord of the Future of Human Race Studies at Pretentious University. And, sadly, Dr. Moxley turns out to be awful. He's a total bore. He's clueless about the audience. He's full of himself, doesn't make eye contact, speaks with endless pauses and umms and uhhs, and reads exclusively off of his very boring slides. He's wearing a leopard-print bathrobe that hasn't been washed in weeks, and he even goes so far as to talk about his pet poodle Poochie's medical issues for five long minutes. It's perhaps the worst lecture you've attended in your life. The lecture ends, and with notable speed you head for the door.

Suddenly, you realize you left your jacket on the chair, so you turn around to go back. When you turn, the dreaded Dr. Moxley is right behind you. With a big smile, he puts his hand on your shoulder and asks, "So, what did you think?" You know exactly what you want to say. Do you say it?

If you're like most people, you would not be honest. I certainly wouldn't. Being honest invites a long conversation or hurt feelings, neither of which I want to cause. I'd want to leave, and the fastest way to achieve that is to play nice. Perhaps you'd hide behind suspicious compliments like, "It was interesting" or "It was fine." Odds are good you'll nod your head affirmatively and smile as you do, hoping to escape. When talking to a performer after his performance, most people will say nice, simple, positive things.

As a result, there are thousands of bad public speakers running around under the impression that they're doing OK. The feedback loop for speakers is broken, and they have simply never been told (in friendly but firm, clear terms) they did not perform well, much less how they can improve. Like singers in the early rounds of *American Idol* who sincerely can't believe they're not the next Whitney Houston or Frank Sinatra, many people live inside a bubble of denial. They've heard enough polite compliments to safely ignore any painful truths that slip through. They may even jab back, decreasing the odds that people will offer any future critiques. Considering how much we like to talk, we suck at both being honest with others and at listening openly and nondefensively when others are honest with us.

One reason we're not fully honest is because we don't want to appear rude. I suspect in your imagined version of Dr. Moxley's lecture, you probably gave him a round of applause when he finished. What is that about? No matter how poorly someone performs, we pay respect for his willingness to even try by applauding his efforts. It's the polite thing to do, and if you saw people who didn't applaud at all, you'd think they were snobs, independent of how good or bad the speaker was. How bad would someone have to do in a lecture to earn zero applause? I've never seen this happen. And since many people see applause as validation that they did well, they will always be satisfied. They step off the stage, ask a friend, "How did I do?", are told, "You did fine," and move on.

Even if you do find people who give you honest feedback and you listen carefully to it, the challenge isn't over. It turns out, we're all too easily deceived.

## The sneaky lessons of Dr. Fox

In 1973, researchers at the University of Southern California hypothesized that students' feedback about their professors was based on nonsense. To test the hypothesis, they conducted an experiment.[2] They hired an actor who "looked distinguished and sounded authoritative" to give a lecture. They gave him a fictitious but impressive resume, and instructed him to use double talk, contradictory statements, and meaningless references. The actor was instructed to be charismatic and entertaining, but to deliberately provide no real substance, including citing books and research papers that did not exist. The actor (aka Dr. Fox) delivered an hour lecture, followed by a half-hour of discussion and Q&A, similar to the format of most university lectures. Afterward, the 11 attendees, who were not merely college students but professionals in the field, were surveyed for their opinions. The table below lists the results.

| Question | Percent agreed |
| --- | --- |
| Did he dwell upon the obvious? | 50 |
| Did he seem interested? | 100 |
| Did he use enough examples? | 90 |
| Did he present in well-organized form? | 90 |

---

2   Naftulin, Donald H., John E. Ware, Jr., and Frank A. Donnelly, "The Doctor Fox Lecture: A Paradigm of Educational Seduction," *Journal of Medical Education*, Vol. 48 (1973): 630–635.

| QUESTION | PERCENT AGREED |
| --- | --- |
| Did he stimulate your thinking? | 100 |
| Did he put his material across in an interesting way? | 90 |
| Have you read any of his publications? | 0 |

The data from this study is sparse, as there were only 11 participants, and it has been criticized for various reasons.[3] However, I buy the conclusions. First, these scores are very good. Any speaker would be proud to see numbers like these. And since these questions are similar to the ones used on conference surveys, it seems that there's something very wrong going on here. How could an actor so easily fool people who were professionals in the same field?

The easy conclusion is that people are bad at detecting bullshit, which is probably true.[4] The more interesting but lazy answer is that to do well at public speaking, you simply have to pretend to know what you're doing. I think that's wrong. This actor likely prepared more intensely than most public speakers do. The fact that he came off as credible was no accident—he studied and practiced to appear that way. I suspect it would have taken the actor less time to prepare to deliver a proper lecture. If anything, this experiment makes the case for a speaker to put in the effort to do a good, honest job.

This research also indicates that what people want from lectures is different from what they say they want, or what the organizers want them to want. The authors of the study point this out:

> *Teaching effectiveness is difficult to study since so many variables must be considered in its evaluation. Among the obvious are the education, social background, knowledge of subject matter, experience, and personality of the educator. It would seem that an educator with the proper combination of these and other variables would be effective. However, such a combination may result in little more than the educator's ability to satisfy students, but not necessarily educate them.*

---

3  Basic complaints about the study include: the sample size is small, the video of the lecture cannot be found, and the survey questions aren't extensive. However, the study has been reproduced successfully and is generally supported by other researchers in the field. See *What's the Use of Lectures?*, Donald A. Bligh (Jossey-Bass), p. 202.

4  One of my most popular essays ever is "How to detect bullshit": *http://www.scottberkun.com/essays/53-how-to-detect-bullshit/*.

What I take from this quote is that people expect very little from most teachers. When listening to a lecture, most people are quite happy to just be entertained (being entertained is often more than people expect to get from any lecture). Learning, as a child or an adult, is often dreadfully boring, making laughter during the learning process a gift. Having likeable and interesting teachers is also rare, and quite pleasant, even though traditionally it's seen as indirectly related to their ability to teach you something. Either way, a speaker can satisfy many audiences without providing much substance, provided he keeps them entertained and interested. Throw a good comedian into the middle of a boring academic conference, and despite his complete ignorance of the subject, I bet he'd score well above average in the feedback.

From experience at failing to do it, I can say that keeping an audience entertained and interested for an hour is quite difficult. Anyone who can deserves respect. But this is not the same achievement as teaching a skill or telling an inspiring story. The best teachers use entertainment as a way to fuel teaching, not simply to make their students laugh.

Other lessons to learn from Dr. Fox:

- **Credibility comes from the host.** If the host says, "This is an expert on X," people will believe it. People are willing to assume credibility based on how and by whom the speaker was introduced. If Dr. Fox gave the same lecture on a random street corner, without the endorsement of a major professional conference or a well-respected member of a community, he'd be ignored. The Dr. Fox experiment can be seen as a study in how we gauge credibility more than how we judge teaching.

- **Superficials count.** Dr. Fox played the part very well, and as a speaker, you need to do the same. Your appearance, manner, posture, and attitude matter. Every audience expects certain superficial things, and if you deliver them, the rest of your job is easier. As credible as you might be, your audience will also judge you on the local flavor of superficial signals of credibility (e.g., don't wear a suit when presenting to a Silicon Valley software company, and skip your favorite tiger-print robe when speaking to CEOs of NYC banks).

- **Enthusiasm matters.** At the moment you open your mouth, you control how much energy you will give to your audience. Everything else can go wrong, but I always choose to be enthusiastic so no one can ever say I wasn't trying hard. The more I seem to care, the more likely people in the audience will care as well. One factor hinted at by the Dr. Fox experiment is that giving significant energy will always help you. By being enthusiastic and caring deeply about what you say, you may provide more value than a low-energy, dispassionate speaker who knows 10 times more than you do. You are more likely to keep the audience's attention, which makes everything else possible.

## Why most speaker evaluations are useless

Most organizers never bother to collect feedback from the attendees, and of those who do, often it doesn't get passed on to the speakers. It's a shame because it's most appropriate for the organizers to share feedback with the speakers; after all, they invited them to speak, so technically the speakers work for the hosts. But being as busy as they are, the organizers don't always communicate the gathered data back to the speakers. They ask the good speakers to come back and leave the rest to figure out life for themselves.

Some do provide feedback, and Figure 8-1 shows a typical report for a speaker at an event. This is real data from a real event, and the speaker was me.

| Session | Very dissatisfied | Somewhat dissatisfied | Neutral | Somewhat satisfied | Very satisfied | Total responses |
|---|---|---|---|---|---|---|
| Making Things Happen | 1 | 3 | 29 | 58 | 38 | 129 |

*Figure 8-1. My scorecard from a recent speaking engagement.*

At first glance, this looks good. Apparently 58 of the 129 people who responded were "Somewhat satisfied." That doesn't sound too bad. I even managed to score a "Very satisfied" from 38 additional people. But a rating of "Neutral" from 29 people is worthless. I'd rather they were forced to decide—if they're not sure where they stand, I'd consider them dissatisfied. Or perhaps they dozed off. That would actually be fascinating data to know: how many people fell asleep during the lecture? (That's a stat I'd love to see at all lectures, especially in universities.)

But the single most valuable data point is how my scores compare to other speakers. Without it, this feedback is useless. Perhaps my scores are the worst of all scores in the history of presentations at this organization. Or perhaps they're the best. There is no way to know. And what about the one guy who was very dissatisfied? Was he important? Maybe he's the VP of the division so his opinion matters more than the others. Or is he, like my former boss, always dissatisfied by everything? Maybe he has never given a score other than "Very dissatisfied." Or perhaps he showed up in the wrong room and thought I'd be speaking about his favorite topic, which to his dismay I never mentioned. Reading this report keeps me mostly in the dark.

The most useful feedback conveys what the dissatisfied people wish I had done differently, and what the satisfied people want me to make sure I do next time. Even if all 129 said they were beyond very dissatisfied, and unanimously agreed on a law banning me from ever speaking again, I wouldn't know what it was that dissatisfied them. I'd have to guess at what changes to make to do better next time, once my appeal goes through and I'm put on speaking probation.

And then, of course, since there were 500 people in the room, what did the other 371 think about my talk? I'll never know. Because only a minority of attendees fill out speaker surveys, the responses typically represent the top and bottom of the feedback curve. Those who passionately love or hate you are best represented because they're the most motivated to participate. The moderate majority is least represented. Since surveys are black holes—no one is informed who exactly will read them, and how they affect the future—there's little reason for most people to be thoughtful about what they say.[5]

---

5  I ran training events at Microsoft for years, and promised that I would personally read every answer submitted in surveys. If people aren't sure who will read their feedback, why would they spend 5 or 10 thoughtful minutes giving it? They won't. Perhaps the surveys will go straight to the trash; who knows? If you don't make someone accountable and visible, you're encouraging people to be cynical of surveys and they will not take them seriously, if they do them at all.

Without a wise, patient hand reviewing the data, it's easy to mis-interpret what it means or how the speaker could have possibly done a better job. Most of the time, the questions in the survey are framed wrong, setting up misinterpretations no matter who gives feedback.

Here's some of the real feedback speakers need:

- How did my presentation compare to the others?
- What one change would have most improved my presentation?
- What questions did you expect me to answer that went unanswered?
- What annoyances did I let get in the way of giving you what you needed?

No matter what data is provided to a speaker, it's easy and free to simply ask people in the audience when you see them afterward. When someone gives you a polite, "Great job!", say, "Thanks, but how could I have made it better?" Get them to move beyond pleas-antries and think for a moment. Give them your business card to encourage them to continue the discussion. After the event, ask your host the aforementioned questions and see what data he'll share with you. Even if he doesn't have data from the audience, he can give his own opinions, which can be just as valuable.

## The speaker must match the audience

What would happen if, in 1942, I booked Mussolini to speak in London? Mussolini was a passionate, perhaps excellent, speaker. But what do you think his survey results would look like? Instead of evaluating Mussolini, the only thing the survey scores would indicate is that the organizer failed to match the speaker to the audience. Speakers can be set up to fail if they are asked to speak to people who hate them, or on a topic they do not care about. I spoke once at Cooper Union, an elite, world-famous university in New York City, where all admitted students get full scholarships. I was on a book tour promoting one of my books. The talk I'd prepared was about all the things that go wrong on projects and how a wise leader can handle them. It was good material, and I'd presented it well many times. But when I arrived, I learned my audience was made up entirely of freshmen: 18- and 19-year-olds without any real-world adult experience. It was October, so they'd been out of high school for maybe five months. I knew instantly, minutes before I was to speak, I was Mussolini in London. Unless I did something drastic, they'd ignore or heckle me as if I were a boring, out-of-touch, manager-loser type—the same way I would have if, at 19, I'd had to sit through a lecture about life in the corporate world.

A savvy speaker must ask the host, "What effect do you want me to have on this audience?", and a good host will think carefully about that answer. And if he doesn't, the speaker may very well be able to figure this out, or interact enough with people in the audience to sort out what they want to get out of the lecture itself. Most of the time people are asked to speak, they say yes without knowing why they were asked or what they are expected to achieve.

During my talk at Cooper Union, I did my best to remember my perception of the adult world when I was 18. So, I dropped my slides, opened with a personal story of my experiences working at Microsoft, and joked about how I met Bill Gates in an elevator (I said hello and he basically ignored me), which earned some mild laughs. I scored an ounce of respect and grew it into a lively Q&A that lasted the hour. I was lucky to pull this off; had I initially asked some basic questions of the host, I would have been prepared from the beginning.

Sometimes the goal is a deliberate mismatch. The host wants a challenging presentation that will inform people of opinions they don't want to hear to rile them up. That's fine, provided at least the host and the speaker are in agreement and whatever survey is done takes this into consideration. Satisfaction means something very different if the goal was to provoke rather than merely to please.

This points out the real challenge in evaluating speakers. Whoever it is that invites someone to speak to an audience has to sort out:

1.  What they (the organizer) want from the speaker.
2.  What the audience wants from the speaker.
3.  What the speaker is capable of doing.

If these three things are not lined up well, the survey will always have problems (e.g., Mussolini in London). If they are aligned, the questions used to evaluate the speaker should be public.

Everyone—the speaker, the audience, and the organizer—should know how the speaker is going to be evaluated. Then the speaker will know in advance and can prepare, much like Dr. Fox, to do whatever he can to score well on those evaluations. Rarely does the audience get a say in surveys, but they should be helping the organizer form the questions.

Better questions to ask attendees include:

- Was this a good use of your time?
- Would you recommend this lecture to others?
- Are you considering doing anything different as a result of this talk?
- Do you know what to do next to continue learning?
- Were you inspired or motivated?[6]
- How likeable did you find the speaker?
- How substantive did you find the speaker's material?

Those last two questions sort out the Dr. Fox dilemma of how well liked speakers were versus how much substance attendees felt the speaker offered them. And if you really want to know the value of a speaker, ask the students a week or a month later. A lecture that might have seemed amazing or boring five minutes after it ended could have surprisingly different value for people later on. If the goal is to change people's behavior in the long term, you have to study the long-term impacts of whatever lectures or courses people are taking.

## Expert feedback you can get right now

As cautious as we are about giving other people tough criticism, we're even more terrified of receiving it. However, it's quite easy today to get feedback on public speaking. In fact, you can do this right now:

1. Grab a video camera.
2. Open your notes or slides for a talk you know (the Gettysburg Address works in a pinch).
3. Videotape yourself presenting it.

---

6 This may matter more than how much they learned.

Five minutes will do just fine. Imagine you have an audience on the wall opposite you, who you should be making eye contact with, and go for it. Then sit down, perhaps with your favorite alcoholic beverage (or seven), and watch. Despite how easy this is to do, most people, even those who say public speaking is important and want to get better at it, aren't willing to do it. It's just too scary for them. To which I say, you are a hypocrite. If you're too scared to watch yourself speak, how can you expect your audience to watch you? The golden rule applies: don't ask people to listen to something you haven't listened to yourself. Just do it. If it's unwatchable, be proud you only inflicted a rotten talk on yourself and not an innocent audience. You can delete the video. You cannot delete an hour of wasted time from people's lives.

We all hate the sound of our own voice. We scrutinize the shape of our nose or our hairline in ways most people never would. Besides, those are things that are difficult to change. It's the other things—how comfortable you seem, how clear your points are, any minor annoyances of body language or diction—that are radically easier to improve.

If you don't like what you see, make it shorter. Go for 30 seconds—short, commercial-length material—and practice it until you can do it well. Then add more. If something feels consistently stupid, take it out and repeat. You will always get better each time you practice something, even if it seems otherwise.

I don't watch video of every talk I do, but if during a talk it doesn't feel right, or something goes really well, I'll go back and watch. When I get feedback from an event organizer that's difficult to interpret, I'll compare it with the videotape. I always want to match my sense of how it felt to me to what it actually looked like to the audience. Pro athletes rely on watching films of their games to see what actually happened (Fred didn't play any defense) instead of what they think happened (Fred blames the rest of his team for not playing any defense).[7] There's too much going on when you're doing an intense activity like sports or

---

7  "There is only one way to stay on top of it: when you watch it on films. Only then can the players and coaches see what went wrong. There are no make-believes with the films, and sometimes it takes a couple of viewings before it sinks in." —Chuck Daly, former Detroit Pistons head coach. Quoted in Ron Hoff's *I Can See You Naked* (Andrews McMeel Publishing), where he offers similar advice.

speaking to be fully aware of what's happening as it happens. Use technology to help show you what you actually did. If you're intimidated by critiquing yourself, make the video and give it to a trusted friend who you know will give you honest, constructive feedback. Keep in mind that a webcam is a tool orators and speakers throughout history would have loved to have had. It's simple, fast, cheap, and private. You can get instant feedback from people nearby or far away, making it easier than ever to experience what it's like to be in your own audience.

## CHAPTER 9

# The clutch is your friend

After years of studying learning theory, the science of how we learn, I can tell you this: most of what you need to know is easily learned from what happened to me in 1989 when I almost killed three people.

The long list of very stupid things not to do in life includes this: making a left turn into three lanes of oncoming traffic, during a driver's test at age 17, in NYC, in your grandmother's old car, during rush hour, while suddenly realizing you never practiced making a left turn into traffic. And in 1989 I did it with predictably disastrous results. Less than a minute into my driver's exam, when asked to make a left turn, I waited behind the car in front of me and then executed a clever move: mimicked the exact action of that car. But the Ford Mustang I followed flew through the intersection several seconds faster than my grandmother's old Honda Civic could manage. Whereas he beat the oncoming traffic and roared on down the road, I ended up directly in the path of a speeding 18-wheel Mack truck.

I remember the look of surprise on the truck driver's face as he slammed on his brakes. He wasn't angry—he didn't have time to be. Instead, he had the focus of adrenalized self-preservation, using every inch of the pedal to discover exactly how effective those brakes were. In the same instant, there was a scream from Mr. Dinko, the scrawny test examiner in the passenger seat. It was a girlish cry of shock, fear, and helpless outrage at the sight of the truck heading straight at him. The clipboard he had been staring at moments earlier flew from his hands across the dashboard, as he screamed something I couldn't understand. Despite being the cause of the chaos, I was surprisingly calm. After all, I'd never done this before. Maybe making left turns into traffic always felt like this.

The truck, after skidding into the intersection and dropping boxes of cargo onto the street, stopped a few feet from the front right corner of my bumper, the bumper of a car entirely in his lane. The intersection was blocked and traffic stopped in both directions. Soon there was shouting and pointing, somehow mostly at the truck driver, and he, like all good New Yorkers, yelled in return. I sped away, not fully aware of how close I'd come to killing three people in a head-on collision. I was so confused that I didn't understand why the examiner was in a rush to get back to the test center only 90 seconds after the driving test began. Left turn, right turn, left turn, he yelled. In the parking lot, with Mr. Dinko screaming as he fled the car, I finally realized I'd failed my driving test. For weeks until I could take the test again, I lived in shame among family and friends—all of whom had passed the test on their first try.

Somehow, I passed the second time. And when I got home, relieved as can be to put it all behind me, my older brother took me aside and said, "You are going to learn to drive stick shift." To which I confidently replied, "No fucking way." I wasn't stupid. The last thing I wanted was to attempt learning something else related to driving. *To try to learn creates the possibility to fail.* And I had only recently recovered from a major, near felonious, catastrophe. Students are always at more risk than their teachers, which helps explain some students' delinquent behavior. They are afraid of failing, or being criticized and embarrassed in front of the class, so they reject the teacher first. And teachers, ironically, are terrified of being ignored by their students, explaining their often totalitarian and self-defeating behavior. In my case, knowing friends and adults who hadn't grasped how to drive stick shift, I didn't want to risk more failure.

But he insisted. He told me to trust him. And down the street we went to his shiny '84 Honda Prelude, the coolest car any of our friends had. That Prelude was his life. He shoved me in the driver's seat and put the key in the ignition. And what did I do? I reached for the door handle to escape. It's one thing to nearly crash your grandmother's car, but if you crash your older brother's car, he'll beat the crap out of you for the rest of your life. I scrambled for excuses—I'm too busy (lie), I'm tired (lie), my feet hurt from the road test (bad lie)—but before anything good came to mind, he said these invaluable words: "The clutch is your friend."

How could the clutch be my friend? The clutch is the weird pedal that almost no one I knew could figure out. The clutch was why kids who tried to learn stick shift lurched around the high school parking lot, stalling their cars while onlookers laughed. The clutch was a thing of evil, a thing to be feared. The clutch being my friend made no sense. What next, Mr. Dinko is my friend? The SATs are my friend? "What the hell are you talking about?", I asked.

And he said, "Trust me, the clutch is your friend. It's there to help you. If you get stuck, just push it all the way down and you'll be OK. If you know this, learning to drive stick isn't hard." I gave him a long look. Was this a trick? But my brother wouldn't do that. Not with his car. Not with me in the driver's seat of his car. So, I said to myself, "OK, maybe the clutch is my friend. Let's see what happens."

Within an afternoon, I was driving manual transmission. I even made a left turn safely into traffic. I was the first kid I knew who could do it, and I learned to love it so much I still drive manual transmission to this day.

What magic did my brother possess that my driving instructors did not? Before we can sort that out, we have to explore why teaching is almost impossible and how what he achieved is rare.

## Why teaching is almost impossible

I'm skeptical about teaching even though I do it for a living. For every good teacher you've had in your life, how many bad ones did you suffer through? Would you say the ratio of good to bad is 1 to 5? 1 to 10? Even in my story above, I suffered the larger failure of three months of professional driving instruction, plus my part-time instructing father, and I still was not prepared for the actual driving test. Or perhaps I failed them. Either way, most attempts at teaching fail. Blame the teachers, blame the students, or blame them both, but most attempts do not satisfy anyone.

I've taught in many formats. Semester-long university courses, full-day seminars, half-day workshops, tutoring sessions, lectures, on-the-job employee mentoring, even drunken barroom tirades, and I can say the odds of learning in any situation are slim. In any moment in any learning environment, where there's one person "teaching" and a bunch of people "learning," I'd wager that 5% are asleep and 25% are thinking about sex. Another 30% are day-dreaming about something else entirely. Of the remaining 40%, some will be in the wrong room and others will be distracted by text messages or emails.[1] And of the tiny percentage of people

---

[1] More optimistically, the particular individuals in a room who are distracted change over time. So, while I do think 30% of people are distracted, it's not the same people all the time. The attention of the room is always changing.

truly paying attention, how many will understand what the teacher is saying? How many will remember it the next day? And of those, how many will even try to apply what they learned in their lives?

All successful teachers must consider these four important questions:

- How many understand?
- How many will remember later?
- How many try to apply the lesson in the real world?
- How many will succeed?

If you set about trying to teach, whether through lectures, classes, or even writing, you will be doing one of the most difficult and frustrating things a person can do with other people. Do not watch films like *Dead Poets Society* with Robin Williams or *Stand and Deliver* with Edward James Olmos. These films do not show the misery and boredom that went on in all the other classrooms, where dull, uninspiring teachers fail distracted students day after day after mind-numbing day. Nor does it show all the bad experiences the teachers endured and fought through to become the (semifictional) brilliant teachers the films portray. Ever wonder why many schoolteachers seem so tired, so mean, so burnt-out on life? They didn't start that way. Teaching anything year after year, while watching so many students struggle to grasp your lessons, eats away at your soul and can't help but overtake the love that drove you to teach in the first place. Most schoolteachers don't even have the chance to burn out: 50% of schoolteachers in the United States do not last more than five years.[2] In the United States, most teachers are paid so little to do so much.

## How to teach anyone anything

There is some very good news: when it works, teaching is one of the most rewarding experiences there is. Seeing an idea you've explained be understood and successfully applied by someone is unlike any other pleasure in life. Even knowing you've reached 5 people out of 100 is worth the disappointment of not reaching the other 95. Had you not shown up that day, you'd never have even reached those five. And maybe the person who would have shown

---

[2] *http://retainingteachers.com/*

up to teach had you chickened out would have only reached three students, or none. Sometimes in life, 5 out of 100 is above average. Besides, there is no alternative to the challenges of teaching—if you want to impart ideas and knowledge, it's the only game in town.

And despite my skepticism and my fluency in depressing statistics, I believe anyone can teach anyone anything. But I mean this in a specific sense. If you have two dedicated, reasonably intelligent people, one interested in teaching and the other wanting to learn, something great can happen. Think master and apprentice, mentor and protégé. For learning, small numbers win. The success of this one-on-one method is proven throughout history; many so-called prodigies were tutored by a parent or family friend (Einstein, Picasso, and Mozart all qualify). Yes, they had amazing, inherent talent, but they were still privately taught by people invested in their learning. Teaching is intimacy of the mind, and you can't achieve that if you must work in large numbers.

Basic math supports this. If I lecture to 5,000 people, I can't know much about any of them. People have different learning styles, and when I speak to an audience of 5,000, I have to average out those differences. I can generalize and make good guesses, but I'm distributing my energy across the entire group. Some lecturers are very good at these guesses, and their concepts resonate with large numbers of people. These lucky few would make for good entertainers or comedians. But for most, it's only as the audience gets smaller—100, 50, 5, and perhaps optimally 1 single student—that a teacher's real power surfaces. You can inform a group of 5,000. You can entertain them. You can offer them new ways to think or ideas to consider, but you can't teach them skills or give them a personalized experience. My brother could not have taught me how to drive stick shift if he were lecturing to 4,999 other people as well. It would have been impossible for him to simultaneously sit in the passenger seat in every one of those cars and watch what each of us did, not to mention give each of us the exclusive attention we would need to learn something new.

With a small group, a good teacher can study each student and determine what she knows, what interests her, and what she fears. Based on that knowledge, the teacher makes adjustments to improve the odds of getting his students over the four challenges I listed previously. A smaller number of students makes it easier for a teacher to be an active, responsive leader; lecturing to a large audience usually requires the instructor to play out a rigid and predefined set of lessons, no matter how little the students understand. Lecturers are fond of saying, "Are there any questions?" to a sea of 100 faces, as if the people who feel lost are willing to embarrass themselves in front of the others who seemingly get it. It's not a forum designed for in-depth one-on-one interaction, which is what has always been necessary for teaching to happen.

There are three things my brother did that anyone trying to teach must do, and it's no surprise that they're easier to do with a smaller number of students:

1.  Make it active and interesting.
2.  Start with an insight that interests the student.
3.  Adapt to how the student responds to #1 and #2.

The bad news: applying these rules always takes more time. The good news: any time at all you spend pays off.

## Active and interesting

This old quote comes up often, and it's a good one:

> *I hear and I forget. I see and I remember. I do and I understand.*

It's attributed to Confucius, but as is true with many famous quotes, it's been told so often by other famous people—such as Benjamin Franklin and Jean Piaget—that they are often credited with the saying instead. Strangely, despite this idea being thousands of years old and having enthusiastic support from brilliant people, few public speakers apply this wisdom. The reason: as difficult as lecturing is, giving the audience things to do is much more difficult.

The best research on learning suggests that the necessary shift is to switch from a teacher-centric to an environment-centric model. Most teachers focus on their lesson plans: what to include in their lectures, what textbooks or software to use, or where in the room they should stand. The teacher is the center of the universe. By contrast, the best teachers focus on the students' needs. They strive to create an environment where all the pieces students need—emotional confidence, physical comfort, and intellectual curiosity—are present at the same time. The teacher has to get out of the way; instead of being the star, he is the facilitator who helps students gain experience. The teacher can achieve this through exercises, games, and challenges where he plays a supporting rather than a primary role.

As Donald A. Bligh advises in his book, *What's the Use of Lectures?* (Jossey-Bass):

> *If you want to teach a behavior skill, at some stage the student should practice it. If you are training athletes to run 100 meters, at some point in that training they should practice running 100 meters.... You might think this principle is obvious. And so it is to ordinary people. But it is quite beyond some of the most intelligent people our educational system has produced.*

For people who have spent years trying to be great public speakers, this opposes what all their hard-earned confidence suggests. They've been fighting to be the center of attention and are proud of the various skills they've attained for doing so. This explains why many professors and gurus who are fantastic lecturers are somehow awful teachers. When their "students" leave, they don't know how to apply anything they heard in the lecture. Given the lecturer's brilliance, the students assume they are the problem and give up.

All solutions to this problem start with the teacher being comfortable doing things other than lecturing. One possibility is to create exercises for your students to practice specific skills, then divide them into small groups so they can collaborate and apply the ideas explained in the lectures to situations similar to those they'll face in the real world.[3] My brother did the right thing from the first moment: he put me in the driver's seat. Whatever happened next would have to happen through me, with his instruction. People never fall asleep if they are at the center of the experience.

Even with large crowds, there are ways to invite people to let you know when they're lost. In Ken Bain's excellent book, *What the Best College Teachers Do* (Harvard University Press), he tells the

---

[3]  There are many compendiums of exercises you can buy. They're handy references. The problem is that off-the-shelf exercises feel just that way to students, and it's important to customize and develop them to fit the students and the goals of your particular course. Start with *Games Trainers Play*, Edward Scannell and John Newstrom (McGraw-Hill). Practice exercises with friends before inflicting them on anyone else.

story of Professor Donald Saari, a mathematician from the University of California, who uses the WGAD ("Who Gives A Damn?") principle. On the first day of class, Professor Saari informs students that they can ask this question at any moment, and he will do his best to explain how whatever obscure thing he's talking about connects to why they signed up for the course. If your goal is to keep people interested, give them permission to let you know when they're having trouble following and are about to tune out. A speaker who wants to teach should see this kind of question not as a sign of failure, but as an opportunity. They're getting real-time information that at least one person isn't following, and if one isn't following, odds are good that others aren't either. If you want real feedback on how to make your material better, find that person after the class and investigate: was there another way to reach him? You have nothing to lose by asking a student the simple question, "How could I have made this lesson more effective for you?"

One tactic is to make your audience members' minds feel active even if their bodies are not. Our brains have *mirror neurons*, and though we don't fully understand how they work, they respond when we see people do things in exactly the same way we would if we were doing them ourselves. This is why when some men watch the Super Bowl on TV, they mimic the tackles and catches as they sit on their couches. Or why people cower in fear when the guy with the hockey mask jumps out from behind the curtain. When people watch a football game (or an axe-murderer), their neurons fire in exactly the same way they would if the observers were actually playing football (or being chased by an axe-murderer). This has been a shocking discovery for scientists, but it makes sense given our activity-prone brains. Even when inactive—say, slouched in the back row of a lecture hall—our brains are so eager to activate, they will respond to the right kind of stimuli. Good storytellers are said to engage or captivate an audience; perhaps mirror neurons are part of what's going on.[4] If you can find great, relevant stories to tell or show in short movies, you can get people's brains firing actively, even if they're still just seated in the audience.

---

4  Scientists are still figuring it all out, but a good summary can be found here: *http://www.pbs.org/wgbh/nova/sciencenow/3204/01.html*.

## Start with an insight of interest

In *What the Best College Teachers Do*, Ken Bain writes:

> Teachers have argued that students cannot learn to think, to analyze, to synthesize, and to make judgments until they "know" the basic facts of the discipline. People in this school of thought have tended to emphasize the delivery of information to the exclusion of all other teaching activities. They seldom expect their students to reason (that will supposedly come after they have "learned the material"). On their examinations, these professors often test for recall, or simple recognition of information (on a multiple choice test for example).

If instead of learning from my brother, I had taken a course on driving manual transmission automobiles, the instructor would have taught me about how transmissions work, the history of transmissions, why they have five gears, the names for each and every part of the dashboard, and on and on. Often what we're taught in school is from an academic and theoretical view of the world. Teachers and academics tend to be people who like to study things, so they naturally encourage their students to study them as well, including things that are better learned by *doing* rather than studying.

Focusing on facts and knowledge makes it easy for the teacher to stay in control and at the center of the experience. In reality, the ability to do something only has a limited relationship to the quantity of knowledge you have. Simply because a teacher knows the names of all these things doesn't mean it has any value to the student or to the skill the student is there to learn. If I'd taken a course on driving manual transmission, it could be weeks before I got in a car, or months until the final exam when I could prove that I knew what to do. Instead, in the first minute of day one, my brother put me in the driver's seat and began his teaching from there.

The phrase, "The clutch is your friend," will stay with me forever. I say it to myself when writing, when planning a workshop, and even before I get on stage to give a big lecture. It reminds me that there is always a way—if I'm as much of an expert as I think I am—to forge a path for anyone to follow into a subject or skill. If I can't make that path, I don't understand my topic as much as my ego thinks I do.

Finding and simplifying insights requires humility, something rarely attributed to experts and public speakers. Keep your hard-earned knowledge in mind, but simultaneously remember how it felt to be a complete novice. It's rare to achieve this balance, but it's what makes a teacher great. It turns out, my brother learned to drive stick the difficult, old-school way. Instead of passing on that misery to me, instead of projecting his own suffering onto me as a rite of passage all drivers should endure, he chose to convert his misery into my delight. Teaching is a compassionate act. It transforms the confusing into the clear, the bad into the good. When it's done well, and the insights are experienced not just by the teacher but by the students as well, everyone should feel good about what's happened. It's amazing how rare it is in many systems for the experience of learning to be a pleasurable thing.

## Adapt to how students respond

If when I got into my brother's car, I had started screaming at the top of my lungs, what should he have done? If he behaved like most speakers do, he'd have continued on with his lesson, never acknowledging my problem. People fall asleep in lectures or stare off into space, but speakers keep right on going. They can get away with this because lectures are a passive experience for the audience.

But if you follow my advice and make the learning process active for your students, they will respond in some way. And that's when your real work begins. If the supposedly brilliant insight you offered bores them, or they don't understand the exercise you planned, what then? The challenge of teaching becomes observing your students, knowing how to respond, and making adjustments to suit their needs.

Even when lecturing, these concepts change how you operate while you're up at the front of the room. You should build your lectures so it is possible to ask yourself, at different points during the presentation:

- Do they know this fact or lesson already?
- Do they need me to explain this point in a different way?
- Are they saturated with information and need a break or a laugh?
- Are they too cocky and need a challenge?

And even if you can't build those things in, nothing stops you from asking your audience, a few days after the lecture (either through the host or by providing a sign-up sheet at your talk where you collect their email addresses):

- Do they have any new questions now that they're back at work?
- Did they use anything you said? What happened?
- Is there a topic that now, since they're back at work/life, they wish you'd covered?
- Can they suggest ways to make the experience they had with you more active, engaging, or interesting?

If you follow this advice, you'll learn it's impossible to teach well without learning something along the way. Good teachers listen as much as they talk, improving their material based on what they hear and studying to see if it had the positive effects they hoped. A bored teacher is merely someone who's forgotten he must keep finding ways to learn from his students, even if it's simply to learn where he has failed them as a teacher.

## CHAPTER 10

# Confessions

**If you want to know how good a speaker really is, watch him give the same lecture twice.** I've studied speakers and comedians, and it's clear they do the same routines hundreds of times to get them right. If you want to learn the secrets of any performer, see his show twice. Then you'll notice how much of what seems improvised truly is. Want to see if that impromptu joke I made was something special or part of the standard routine? You'll only know for sure if you see me twice.

**I've heard your question before.** If I know my material, I've likely considered your question or been asked it before. The problem is, I can't answer all the questions my material might introduce. It would be boring for reasons described earlier in the book. By the third or fourth time I've given a lecture, I've heard 70% of the questions I'll likely ever hear on the topic. But all questions are good questions. Just because I've heard it before doesn't mean I have a great answer yet, so I'm learning no matter how many times I've done it.

**I have trouble making eye contact with friends.** I'm very comfortable speaking to crowds, but if during the talk I see friends, my brain wants to joke with them; however, my instincts know it would be self-indulgent to do so. I love having friends attend my lectures, but part of me freezes when I see them. Not entirely sure why. You'd think I'd have sorted this out by now, but I haven't.

**Half the time you already know what you need to know.** Sometimes people at my talks know much of what I know. In these cases, my value is to remind them of an old idea or put it into a new context. I know I don't have to have original ideas to have value. Often there's value in something that's been said before being said again in a different way, or by someone new who can get away with saying truths insiders can't. Hearing a message from an outsider often carries more weight than a team of expert insiders. But I can't say this. If I mention that I'm deliberately telling you things you've heard before because you need to hear them again, it would be patronizing. Yet I know old ideas said well have surprising power in a world where everyone obsesses about what's new.

**Change only happens when someone does something different, which a lecture cannot do.** Often I'm hired to be inspirational and tell people tales of how great innovations came to be. The problem with inspiration is that it's hard to take with you. What's thrilling in the lecture hall feels awkward in front of your boss. Someone has to leave the lecture, go back to his everyday world, and take the risk of doing something different with what he's learned. No speaker can ensure this happens. Sometimes I'm hired to preach to the choir when the people who most need to hear my message are elsewhere. This is fun, but it's a problem I can't solve since I rarely get to pick my audiences.

**I'm paid the same whether I suck or not.** Most speaking contracts have no performance clauses. Whether I bomb or do amazingly well, I'm paid the same. I don't like this. I'd rather be paid less when I'm bad and more when I'm good. As it stands, there are few performance incentives at conferences. There should be awards for the best speakers based on audience feedback, and coaching offered to speakers who don't do well. The only conference I know that pays speakers based on performance is UIE's User Interface Conference.[1]

**Full-day seminars are misery for teachers and students.** Most of the research points to 9 a.m.–5 p.m., high-volume, short-break, full-day seminars as a bad learning environment. However, that's what people are used to, so that's the way it is. There is no research that says you learn more in eight hours of continuous learning than you do in six. In fact, there's evidence to the contrary.[2] Volume does not equal quality, but we're trained to buy by volume. Unless it's highly interactive, has frequent breaks, and is constructed around real-world situations, not much retention is likely to happen. Seminars from 9 a.m. to 5 p.m. are exhausting; the result of a great teaching experience should feel energizing. Three 90-minute sessions or four 60-minute sessions, with many breaks, is my preferred way to run a full-day experience.

**I'm an introvert.** While I love talking with interesting, friendly people, I'm extremely happy all on my own. If anything, I think people who are at the center of attention when working—like comedians, teachers, and lecturers—are quieter than average off stage. They, like me, exhaust much of their social energy while working. If you have an interesting opinion, laugh often, and bring a nice bottle of wine, I would love to talk with you. But all things equal, I'm extremely happy with a good book and a nice view.

---

[1] *http://www.uie.com*

[2] *What's the Use of Lectures?*, Donald A. Bligh (Jossey-Bass)

**I see everything you do.** I know when you look at your laptop. I know when you play with your cell phone. I can tell where you are looking at all times. In a good room with raised rows, I know in every instant how many pairs of eyes I have on me. I don't want you to know this. I like feedback on how I'm doing. But I can tell who is listening, who is daydreaming, who gets what I'm saying, and who thinks I'm a jackass. I can even often guess who's going to ask me the first question, who wants to come up to talk to me but is too shy, and who wishes they never came at all.

**No matter how much you hate or love this book, you're unlikely to be a good public speaker.** The marketing for this book likely promised you'd be a better speaker for reading it. I think that's true on one condition: you practice (which I know most of you won't do). Most people are lazy. I'm lazy. I expect you're lazy, too. There will always be a shortage of good public speakers in the world, no matter how many great books there are on the subject. It's a performance skill, and performance means practice—and that's one of the reasons I wasn't afraid to write this book.

**Sometimes I lecture commando.** There's an advantage in knowing something the audience does not, provided that advantage—however ridiculous it is—makes me laugh. Perhaps I need more therapy, but I find that doing little things like this makes life fun. And I laugh, so it works. If not wearing underwear doesn't make you laugh, then don't do it. But find something that always makes you laugh. Whatever I have to do so I'm having fun is to the crowd's advantage, even if they don't know why I'm having fun. Even if the private joke is on them, they benefit.

**I'd rather do Q&A for an hour than lecture.** This is the opposite of many speakers I know. I prefer Q&A because it's live. Anything can happen. I can't just go to the next slide, I have to be responding and thinking. If I have a lively crowd, or just a crowd willing to ask tough, direct questions, it's always a good experience. I hate softball Q&A because not only am I bored, but the audience is, too. Great Q&A is memorable, exciting, and has most of the elements people hope for when they come to live events. But many people demand a show. They feel cheated if it's just Q&A. This means giving a lecture needs to be a compromise of satisfying folks who want to passively hear a lecture, and exciting those who want to get involved and make it a big, thrilling conversation.

**I'm one of the worst students in the world.** I hate lectures. It is very difficult for me to sit and listen to anyone lecture. If I see a good speaker, I usually prefer to go and read his blog or buy his book than sit and listen to his entire talk. I'd prefer to buy him coffee or exchange email, where the communication is two ways. If I can't do that, I'd rather go out into the hallway and have a conversation with someone else, sit outside on the grass and watch the clouds, or go for a walk, all active things where my mind can interact or be free to wander. I find the irony of this endlessly entertaining: I'm a public speaker who mostly doesn't like listening to public speaking.

**Paying attention makes things funny.** If I have any secret to being entertaining, it's that I studied improv theater. There I learned how to see and how to listen. Humor and insight come from paying attention, not from special talents. After I studied improv, my speaking skills improved dramatically and my attitude about life changed. I can't recommend taking an improv theater class strongly enough.

**Making connections is everything.** It's preachy as hell, but lovers of wisdom have an obligation to share. E. M. Forster wrote, "Only connect!... Only connect the prose and the passion, and both will be exalted, and human love will be seen at its height." To love ideas is to love making connections. This is why people who bludgeon others with knowledge, intimidate with facts, distort intended meanings, and cherry-pick their examples are so easy to hate. They work against progress. "Only connect" is great advice. If you don't know what you're connecting through your words, you're more selfish than you realize.

**The easiest way to be interesting is to be honest.** People rarely say what they truly feel, yet this is what audiences desire most. If you can speak a truth most people are afraid to say, you're a hero. If you're honest, even if people disagree, they will find you interesting and keep listening. Making connections with people starts by either getting them interested in your ideas or showing how interested you are in theirs. Both happen faster the more honest everyone is. The feedback most speakers need is "Be more honest." Stop hiding and posturing, and just tell the truth.

**If you love ideas, speaking and writing are natural consequences.**
You know about history's great thinkers because they either spoke
or they wrote. Or someone spoke or wrote about what they did
with or without their permission. I hope to be a great thinker
someday, and I know the way to get there is to speak and write.
Expressing ideas is often the only way to fully understand what
ideas are, and to know what it is you really think. Expression
makes learning from the criticism of others possible, and I'm
happy to look like a fool if in return I learn something I wouldn't
have learned any other way. I'm fascinated by ideas of all kinds, in
wildly different subjects, and I hope to write and speak about
them all. I'm insanely grateful to make a living as a trafficker of
ideas. I hope to be able to do it for the rest of my life.

# Backstage notes

# The little things pros do

When you do anything difficult for a living, little things make a big difference. Any reliable advantage I can get is one I always take. Over the years, I've come across some that can help anyone, regardless of how often you speak. Some require help from the venue you're speaking in, but most only demand arriving early and some extra time.

## The confidence monitor

To connect with an audience, I have to make as much eye contact as possible. But this is a challenge when my slides are projected behind me on a screen. To make sure the audience sees what I think they're seeing, I normally have to turn and look at the screen or stay behind the lectern, limiting how much I can move or interact with the crowd. The solution is to use what's called a *confidence monitor*. It's put up at the front of the stage and shows me exactly what's on the screen, which is an enormous advantage (see Figure A-1). First, I don't have to turn around to see what's on my own slide, preventing the rookie mistake of having my back to the audience. Second, I can use my peripheral vision to verify that the slide transition has worked properly without having to look directly at the screen. With a remote control, I can be almost anywhere on the stage and, mid-sentence, advance a slide with a perfect voiceover transition.

*Figure A-1. A confidence monitor where the crowd can't see it.*

PowerPoint and Keynote both have presenter mode features that allow the confidence monitor to show not only the current slide, but also a small version of the next, or even any notes you've prepared.

## The countdown timer

It's very hard to track time while speaking. There are too many things going on simultaneously to remember to check the time and calculate how much remains while giving your lecture. For this reason, big events often place a countdown timer up front next to the confidence monitor. Some of these clocks also have three lights—red, yellow, and green—to indicate how much time is left. Green is how you start, yellow means one or five minutes remain, and red means you're done. You don't need fancy technology to do this. Good hosts hold up paper signs that read, "10 minutes," "5 minutes," and "Wrap it up," as appropriate. Of course, speakers can take care of this themselves if they have the right remote control.

## The remote control

Occasionally, you'll see a speaker so unaware of the value of a remote that he runs back and forth from center stage to the lectern, only for the sake of advancing slides. This is called the "circle of slide death," the circle being made by the speaker on every roundtrip. I used to be that guy. I hated remotes because I thought only pompous, phony salesman-types used them. But I realized over the years that working without a remote was just stupid. Without one, I had to find the mouse or keyboard every single time I wanted my slides to do something, and during that time, my focus switched from the audience to my gear. Any time I have to focus on gear and not my message, I'm making a mistake. Over 20 or 30 slides, the extra work of shifting focus back and forth, and the little clicking sound of the mouse creating an idiotic, unintended soundtrack, can kill whatever flow I worked so hard to get.

Having control in your hand gives you complete freedom. You can do whatever you want at any time—roam the stage, go into the crowd, stand behind the lectern, or make a few points from the last row (but always check with the tech crew, as wireless microphones can create feedback if you leave the stage). Even if you don't do any of those things, your body knows you can and has one less restriction to worry about. Remotes cost $20–40. Why not have one?

The best model I know of is the one recommended by Guy Kawasaki, the Logitech Cordless Presenter (Figure A-2). Its only downside is it's so big it's hard to hide even in my large hands, but everything else is done right. It has a built-in timer that will vibrate as an alarm, letting you know when you're running out of time.

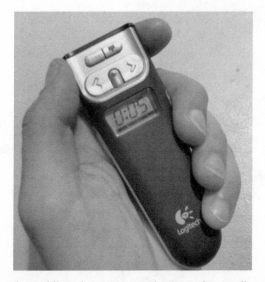

*Figure A-2. The Cadillac of remote controls: Logitech's Cordless Presenter.*

## Give stuff away to fill the front row

The front row at lectures is like the Bermuda Triangle. No one wants to sit there for fear of being embarrassingly bored or not being able to escape. But as described in Chapter 4, I want a dense crowd, and I want it most packed where I am, near the stage. This means a full front row works to my advantage. I often bring books to give away during Q&A, but if the front is empty, I offer a free book to anyone who is willing to move to the front. It always works, usually entertains those who are too lazy to move, and makes the audience seem much less threatening to me. (The toughest, scariest people seem harmless when they are chasing after free things.) The more worried I am about a talk, the more likely it is I'll bring books (Figure A-3 shows me with a pile of my books). If you don't have books of your own, nothing stops you from buying good books someone else wrote on the topic you're speaking about and giving those away ($100 is money well spent if it cuts your nerves and loosens up the crowd). The effect will be the same. Do not give away ugly swag and junk. If you offer cheap things that no one wants, your front row will remain empty, and you are stuck with piles of unpopular items you couldn't even give away.

*Figure A-3.* Have good things to offer people to fill the front row. Put them out where they can be seen so it builds curiosity about what you're going to do with them.

## Hide your microphone (and wear a collar)

Most events use wireless microphones, which require clipping a lapel mike to your shirt. I'm not a fan of fancy clothes for lectures (there are better ways of showing respect for audiences), but dress shirts are the best, most reliable way to clip on these microphones. On a sweater or T-shirt, the lapel mike will pinch the fabric, which is easy to notice. The goal of the wireless mike is to be as inconspicuous as possible.

To help with this, you should always run the wire for the microphone under your shirt, instead of letting it dangle over. There are two reasons for this. First, leaving it out looks bad and is distracting. Second, if you talk with your hands as I do, that dangling cable is just asking for trouble. I have, when making a point, caught my thumb on the cord, sending the microphone flying and making loud, awful, embarrassing noises over the PA. You'll notice the difference in Figure A-4.

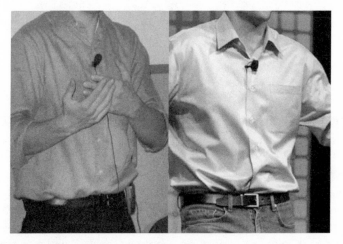

**Figure A-4.** *Tuck your microphone cord under your shirt. The trick is to detach the cord from the box, drop it down your shirt, and reconnect it once it's through your shirt.*

## We don't need no stinking badges

If you are on stage, you can assume you don't need a name tag. People know who you are. You're the one with the microphone. A badge is distracting and can get caught in your hands like the microphone wire. Good hosts catch this before speakers go on and remind them to take off the name tag.

## Lectern vs. podium

It's a gripe among theater types, but the podium is what you stand on. The lectern is what you stand behind. If you want to annoy your public speaking friends, point out every time they say podium when they mean lectern (Figure A-5).

*Figure A-5. Do not stand behind the podium. You will look very silly if you do.*

## Work the camera

These days, many presentations are videotaped, which means it's possible your real audience is not the crowd in front of you. Instead, it's the people who will watch online in the months and years that follow. Many more people watch TED talks over the Internet than attended the conference in California. If you're smart, you will treat your cameramen well. They can do all kinds of things to make you look or sound stupid, so get on their good side. Ask their names, ask their advice, and treat them like people, not servants. When you're preparing, craft your material and slides with the web audience in mind. You're projecting not just to the back row in the room, but to the people who will watch on a tiny window on a computer monitor. Often, people watching online have no sense of how good or bad things were live (the sense of dead air or a tough crowd gets lost on video, which means sometimes you can bomb in real time, but do very well online). When Stephen Colbert presented at former president Bush's press dinner, it was a disaster (it's also a notoriously tough crowd). The room hated him. But the talk was a huge hit on the Web.

# How to make a point

On my way home from Norway last June, I had a layover in Dulles International Airport in Washington, D.C. With hours to kill, jet-lagged out of my mind, I sat in the only comfortable place I could find, a bench next to the United Airlines customer service desk. I couldn't help but overhear the conversations taking place between irate passengers and the under-siege United Airlines service staff. Annoyed at first by the constant arguing, I soon found these dialogs fascinating. Every two minutes, another drama would play out—downtrodden passengers made their cases for something they didn't have but wanted: upgrades, better seats, refunds, or meal vouchers. Sometimes they were simply trying, after long hours stuck in the airport, to get home. After hours of encounters, I recognized three ways people made their cases:

1. United Airlines is wrong.
2. I am special and deserve a seat.
3. I am angry, and you should appease me.

If Aristotle were stuck in Dulles with me, after wondering why no one else was wearing a toga, he'd recognize this list. These three approaches fit what he outlined more than 2,000 years ago for how to make a point. Back in the day this was called *rhetoric*: the ability, in each particular case, to see the available means of persuasion. Most people today only know of the most limited use of the word, as in a rhetorical question (a question asked for effect: "Do you think I want to be stuck in Dulles Airport all day?").

But it turns out the Greeks outlined all the tactics used today by courtroom lawyers, infomercial pitchmen, Sunday preachers, and just about any other person trying to make a point to someone else. In rhetorical terms, the previous list is described as:

1. *Logos*: Logic
2. *Ethos*: Character
3. *Pathos*: Emotion

With this list in mind, you have the basic time-tested toolkit for making a point. Any pitch you make, story you tell, or question you ask uses one of these three elements, and often more than one at the same time. Good presentations hinge on sorting out which approaches will work best with your particular audience. Sadly, on this day in Dulles, I didn't hear any passengers win their cases. They were all turned away. Sometimes there is no way to win, no matter what tactics you use (for the record, there was one bribe, a young woman broke out in tears, and a guy the size of a linebacker threw his backpack on the ground in frustration). Just as on some days, with some audiences, you make your best points and they don't buy them at all.

But when an argument works in a presentation, all the principles come from rhetoric. I learned about rhetoric growing up in my house in Queens, New York. We didn't call it rhetoric, we just called it dinner. Most nights, as we ate our meal, we'd argue about the Cold War, the Yankees, the meanings of various words, and where the safest place in the world would be during a nuclear war. And when we ran out of things to argue about, we'd argue about different ways to argue. My dad loved to argue so much he'd rarely ever admit he was wrong, using various rhetorical tactics to save himself, provoking long debates late into the night. This drove my family crazy but also gave me amazingly thorough lessons on practical rhetoric.

Many well-known phrases from modern advertisements are just simple applications of one kind of rhetoric or another. The famous, "But wait, there's more," found in most infomercials, is called *Dirimens copulatio*, which translates to mean a joining together that interrupts.[1] Tricks like saying, "Are you that stupid?", where you

---

[1] *A Handlist of Rhetorical Terms*, Richard A. Lanham (University of California Press), p. 56.

shift the focus away from the argument and challenge the character of the person making the argument are called *Ad hominem*, which translates to attack the person. It's a trick because even stupid people can make smart arguments now and then, as well as vice versa.

Public speakers unfortunately abuse rhetoric all the time. It's hard to stop them. Since audiences tend to mostly listen and are rarely brazen enough to interrupt a presentation, by the time it's over, they're more likely to want to go home than to question something said 20 minutes earlier. Speakers can intentionally distort, mislead, and even say outright lies, and most of the audience won't do much to stop them—even the people who know more about the subject or rhetoric than the speaker. Many points made in presentations are unsupported, deceptive, or downright made up. It's a sad thing. Filling out feedback forms and writing emails to people questioning what they said is about all we can do.

The most useful inventory of rhetorical tactics I've seen is *Thank You for Arguing*, by Jay Heinrichs (Three Rivers Press). And the best reference on rhetoric never before offered in a public-speaking book is the movie *Animal House*. It contains two speeches that should be studied by all public speakers. In the first, Otter successfully equates banning their fraternity with being un-American, and in the second, Bluto and Otter convince the demoralized fraternity they are just the guys to do a really futile and stupid thing.[2]

Beyond these recommendations, rhetoric is too large a topic to take on in full here; instead, here are much simpler tactics for making your points. And this starts with emphasis.

The first thing, and it's very important that you do this immediately, is to say the following sentence aloud:

> *If Peter Piper picked a purple peck of perpendicular pickled pink peppers, where's the peck of pickled peppers Peter Piper picked?*

---

[2] You can watch these two speeches online at *http://bit.ly/ahouse-ottersdef* and *http://bit.ly/ahouse-blutto*. For greatest effect, read *Thank You for Arguing* first, and note every rhetorical device used and abused in both speeches.

I suspect you struggled with it, as everyone does. This was the point, since it makes the next exercise easy. Now say this non-silly, non-rhyme-based sentence out loud:

*I believe all people should have the right to laugh.*

If you said it in your normal speaking voice, and we charted how much emphasis you placed on any specific word, it would look like Figure B-1, a flat line of equally emphasized words.

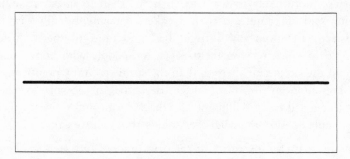

**Figure B-1.** *If this were an EKG, we'd be calling the morgue.*

This is how people often speak when they're nervous—everything is flat and monotone. Even if they're loud, every word is equally loud. They could be talking about the surprise ending of a movie or revealing the secret recipe for Coca-Cola, but their natural energy for the topic is not conveyed in how they're saying what they're saying.

Now say the same sentence again, but emphasize the bold word. Say the bold word twice as loud and twice as long as the others:

*I believe **all** people should have the right to laugh.*

You'd have a chart that looks like Figure B-2.

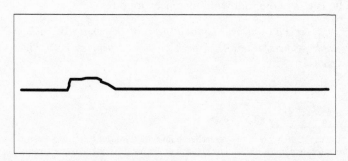

**Figure B-2.** *If this were a patient's EKG, there would be hope.*

You're putting energy into the sentence, and that energy creates a new kind of meaning. You can change the point you are making simply by changing which word you emphasize. Try saying the following sentences, again emphasizing the word in bold[3] by saying it twice as long and twice as loud:

- **I** believe all people should have the right to laugh today.
- I **believe** all people should have the right to laugh today.
- I believe **all** people should have the right to laugh today.
- I believe all **people** should have the right to laugh today.
- I believe all people **should** have the right to laugh today.
- I believe all people should **have** the right to laugh today.
- I believe all people should have **the** right to laugh today.
- I believe all people should have the **right** to laugh today.
- I believe all people should have the right **to** laugh today.
- I believe all people should have the right to **laugh** today.
- I believe all people should have the right to laugh **today.**

Many speakers bury their emphasis. Or they're sloppy, throwing it around like dirty laundry on the floor of a teenager's bedroom. They will score points for putting energy into how they speak, but it's confusing as to why they're doing it when they do. This is better than being flat, but not by much. The goal is to use emphasis to help make each point as clear as possible.

You can listen to any great speaker and break down each sentence he says purely by where he places emphasis. He will use different kinds of emphasis, such as repeating words, pausing, gesturing with his hands, or even speaking with a whisper. There's a whole system of information being given by a good speaker that many people never notice. It's not in the slides. It's not in the thinking. It's in the thoughtful delivery of each sentence he says. Good speakers have a range of emphasis methods, which are easy to spot if you look for them, that improves everything else about their presentations.

---

3  This exercise is based on one found in *Lend Me Your Ears*, Max Atkinson (Oxford University Press), p. 58.

However, much like in life, people with big vocabularies often insist on being magniloquent when it's unnecessary. Public speakers had no microphones or video cameras 150 years ago. They had to be larger than life just so most people watching could see and hear them. But today, anyone who goes too far just looks phony, like they're acting more than presenting (preachers are notorious for using an oratory style that's no longer necessary given the invention of microphones). Being overly dramatic often kills the goal of connecting with an audience.

## Being silent makes your points

Most people say "umm" and "uhh" when they speak. These are called *filler sounds*, and we make them mostly to hold our place in conversation. You're letting the people you're talking to know you are not done speaking. When presenting, this isn't necessary since you're the only one with the microphone, yet we do it anyway, mostly because we're afraid of silence. Standing in front of a room filled with people while doing absolutely nothing feels very strange. And the easy, comfortable, natural way to avoid that feeling is to never let there be silence—simply fill all dead space with "ummm." This is bad. Nothing kills your power over a room as much as a lack of silence.

Silence establishes a baseline of energy in the room. Sometimes when a room is silent, people pay more attention than when you are speaking (a fact many don't know since they work so hard to prevent any silence when speaking). If you constantly fill the air with sounds, the audience members' ears and minds never get a break. If what you are saying is interesting or persuasive, they will need some moments between your sentences and your points to digest. Also, many people take notes, even if just mental notes, and they need time to do that. Filling the space with ummms denies their brains that chance. If you listen to stand-up comedians, about 20–30% of their time on the microphone is spent in silence, often just to let the audience laugh and enjoy the last thing said, or to provide a pacing break to set up the next thing they want to say.

The technical term for what happens when too much information is given to an audience—even if it's in the form of filler sounds—is called *interference*. When point A is still lingering in people's minds, and you hit them over the head with point B, they will inevitably forget some of point A. And when they are trying to think through what you just said in point B, and you're still pretending to talk by saying "ummmm," they don't get the signal that point B has been made and they can digest it.

Donald A. Bligh offers this advice in *What's the Use of Lectures?*:[4]

> *Silence between teachers' remarks is a very important part of a lecture. Silence provides time for consolidation and thought. Their timings requires the skill of an actor. They are useful after rhetorical questions, or when a problem has been posed; provided attention is maintained, they may need to be longer in the third quarter of a lecture, where interference is greatest. Interference is probably the chief cause of forgetting in lectures, particularly when the lecture is too fast.*

Learning to stop saying "umm" requires only one thing: practice. People who speak without saying "umm" weren't born that way. They used to do it and have worked their way out of the habit. If you're not sure whether or not you do it, you most likely do. And you're probably in good company. Many famous politicians, celebrities, and executives are hard to listen to because of their annoying filler sounds. It's an easy problem to have, since fixing it is a simple, fail-safe way to make all of your presentations better.

---

[4] (Jossey-Bass), p. 32.

# What to do if your talk sucks

Should you discover that a talk you are preparing to do, or one you've given before, sucks, this is for you.

While some books on public speaking have long checklists of little things, this is my short checklist of big things. If I see a presentation I think is bad, it's for one or more of the reasons that follow.

## Why your talk might suck

### This is your first time

No one wants to have his brain surgery performed by a rookie. When you step to the front of the room, make sure you don't behave like someone who has never been in the front of the room before, even if it's true. People who are baffled by their own laptops, confused by how their remotes work, or who spend most of their time looking at their own slides with their backs to the audience are indicating they are doing this for the first time. No audience wants to feel they are your dry run, unless somehow your experimenting makes it fun for them (which it probably won't).

**Solution: Practice until it feels good.** Anything you plan to do in your talk must be practiced. If you get a new laptop, remote, or presentation software, give those things trial runs well in advance. Do a dry run in the lecture hall to get used to the space. And work hard on the transitions between slides and points, since this is often where it's easiest to seem lost. When you practice, look to eliminate things that make it seem like you've never done your presentation before (see Chapter 2).

## You are a turtle on crack

Turtles are slow. Turtles on crack are still slow, but they're also unpredictable. They stumble, they stop, and they no longer move in a straight line. Trying to follow a turtle on crack is extremely frustrating. If the pace of your presentation is unclear, or you're not sure what direction you are going in, you are a turtle on crack.[1]

**Solution: Provide a rhythm the audience can follow.** Have a well-defined, simple, uniform pace. Divide your time into the number of points you want to make and spend an equal amount of time on each one. You can subdivide each point into individual arguments, which should also have a clear, simple rhythm to follow. Top-10 lists and frequently asked questions are easy formats to use because they create natural rhythms for your presentation (see Chapter 6). No one is timing you, so if some points need to be longer, that's fine. Just make sure your pace and rhythm makes sense to your audience and not just to you.

## Obfuscation of fractured bilateral rhetoric

People love to sound smart. We love to use the biggest words we know and say the fanciest, most cryptic jargon and acronyms. Doing this makes us feel superior. And when intimidated by an audience, as many professors and experts clearly are, superiority seems to be the best defense. The problem is that no one likes feeling like an idiot. There are 10 million bad, obscure ways to say something for every clear, direct one. If you choose one of the 10 million, no matter how proud it makes you feel to be obscure, you are inviting your audience to start daydreaming. The presentation is now about your fear of making a clear point, rather than about the audience's experience. They should not be doing the hard work—you should. You are up there to share, persuade, or teach,

---

[1] No turtles were harmed in the making of this book, as it appears turtles enjoy crack immensely. (If you work for PETA, this is a joke. If you don't work for PETA, I have a great video to show you.)

and that means you have to drop the defenses, think clearly, and be at the level your audience wants.

**Solution: Clarify your points.** Find simple, clear ways to make your points. If you are a quantum physicist or have 12 PhDs, your arguments and details might be very complex. But are you sure everyone in your audience has 12 PhDs as well? Do you know why they are in the audience and what they hope to learn? If you are speaking to serve your audience and not yourself, every point you make should be understood by most of the room. They might not agree with your points, and they may miss the nuances, but few should be confused about the points you are making and why you are making them (see Chapter 5). Stephen Hawking was at least trying to explain everything in *A Brief History of Time* (Bantam), despite few mortals making it past Chapter 2. If he sees the value in explaining to lesser minds, so can you.

## You make sex boring

Most of us like sex quite a lot. It's a natural fact since we come from an ancestry of people who were required to have sex to get us here. It's the most interesting and exciting primal drive we have. Yet it is still possible for a presentation about sex to be boring. Anyone can kill a topic by speaking in monotone, looking disinterested, picking uninspired examples, and behaving like he doesn't care about what he's saying. If you are not excited and energetic about your message, how can you expect your audience to be?

**Solution: Take an interesting angle from the beginning.** If you choose your topic and opinion, pick something interesting. Take a stand. Force a point of view into the title, and let it grow into the points you make. Even if your topic is only interesting to you, if you express your passion well, the audience will want to follow simply because of your enthusiasm (see Chapter 6).

## Your slides make me hate you

Slides are dangerous. There are so many ways to annoy an audience with slides. Ugly, overloaded, confusing slide decks are common despite how little knowledge they convey, and how much they distract speakers from making their points. There are many kinds of information that cannot be given in a presentation.

We have documents, reports, websites, and movies for good reason. No one wants to read 10-point text off a projector screen. No one wants to try and interpret the 50-element flowchart you've made. It's the wrong medium. Unless slides are essential and the clearest, simplest way to make your point (which they almost never are), use fewer of them. If a prop does not support your point, it has wasted your audience's time.

**Solution: Do not start in PowerPoint; start by thinking about and understanding your audience.** Use visuals and pictures to support the points you want to make. If you put notes in your slides so you don't feel scared, do it in a way that does not annoy your audience. Or instead, have an outline that surfaces in your talk, or bring simple notes on stage with you (see Chapter 5).

## You are afraid of the crowd

We have good reasons for being afraid of audiences. But if fear is the primary thing you feel while speaking, the audience won't enjoy or learn anything. Averting your eyes, hiding behind the lectern, and pacing the stage all indicate you are afraid of the audience, which makes them mostly not want to watch you.

**Solution: Find a way to enjoy yourself.** Bring giveaways to warm the audience up to you and get some easy smiles, which may help you relax. Get there early so you can meet some of the crowd, making them less intimidating. Pick topics you love, so the pleasure of sharing it with others can give you some positive energy to balance out the natural fear you feel.

# Medium list of little things

These are definitely small things, but people are picky. If you do an annoyance often enough, and people notice it, it can distract from all the good things you're doing. No one ever eliminates these issues completely, which is why I keep this list around. If everything else is good, don't worry much about these. But if you want to seem polished and avoid people missing your message for superficial reasons, this list is for you.

There is no way to catch these annoyances unless you watch a videotape of yourself or have someone track these for you while you speak.

- **Umms and uhhs.** These are verbal placeholders. They make sense when talking casually, but when you're speaking to an audience, they're annoying. You can overcome the habit by learning to simply pause in silence. It's unnerving at first to be at the lectern in a silent room, but it creates a new kind of power that is free and easy to get at any time. When the room is silent, all eyes return to you.

- **Distractions and tics.** Little gestures you repeat can be distracting. If you keep rubbing your nose or putting your hands into and out of your pockets, eventually this draws attention away from what you are saying. My nervous tic, as odd as it sounds, is itching the second rib on my right side. Watch enough presentations where I'm talking, and you'll see it about 30% of the time. No idea why I do this (perhaps I still have some chimpanzee genes in me). I do it less now than I used to, but sometimes I still do it.

- **Putting the audience behind you.** You should always avoid showing your back to the audience. If you need to look at your slides, do it from an angle so your audience can still see your face. This is one of the reasons confidence monitors are useful.

- **Repetition.** We all have pet phrases we use too much, like saying, "This is about," "So now...," or "And here we have" to introduce every slide. There are always alternative ways to say the same thing, but first you have to notice which phrases you rely on more than necessary.

- **No eye contact.** Where are your eyes? Rookie speakers look at their shoes, at the same person the entire 60 minutes, or into outer space. At least look at the back of the crowd so that people in the audience will believe you are looking at someone else. The ideal is to look at different parts of the room at different times, paced long enough that it seems natural, even though it never entirely feels that way.

- **Discomfort.** Some people seem very comfortable with their hands in their pockets. Most don't, but so what? Everyone experiences comfort differently. The point is that you need to appear natural enough that people can focus on what you're saying, and you seem happy to be up there. If you constantly stare at the pitcher of water on the edge of the lectern for fear of it falling over, you will seem uncomfortable. So, move it. Don't wear a suit if that makes you miserable, but dress with respect for your crowd. Always err on the side of what will make you more comfortable. If you don't take time to breathe or give pauses for people to consider what you just said, no matter how strong your powers of denial are, you are not yet comfortable speaking.

- **Dispassionate.** One of the basic lessons of the Dr. Fox story in Chapter 8 is that enthusiasm counts. The more you seem to care, even if you don't make sense, the more people will want to understand what it is you're trying to say. Few people speak passionately. They think they're being passionate, but to the audience they come off as only mildly engaging. Watch the video of a passionate speaker (MLK's "I Have a Dream" speech is a good choice), and then watch a video of yourself. Take notes on how to close the difference while still being you.

- **Referenced data.** If research or a study is quoted, it better be referenced somewhere. Saying, "Studies have shown..." but not being able to name at least one source means you are making things up or don't really know what you're talking about.

- **Inappropriate for this audience.** Have the right assumptions been made about who is in the crowd, what they want to know, and what they need to hear?

## Feedback you get for free

If you're giving a presentation in five minutes and you don't have time to videotape yourself, you can still get feedback. As a general rule, what people *do* matters more than what they say or write on feedback forms (and depending on how the survey was constructed, it might be useless anyhow; see Chapter 8).

If my audience does any of these three things, I know I did at least something right:

- **They make eye contact with me.** Every culture has different etiquette about laughter, applause, and even asking questions, but eye contact is universal. The litmus test: if you were to say, "I will give $10 million away to everyone who is looking at me in

five seconds," and count down from five to one, you will get
100% of the audience's attention every time. So it is possible
to win the war against people playing Solitaire on their cell
phones, typing on laptops, or daydreaming if what you say is
interesting enough. It's good to reestablish the attention of the
room every 10 minutes just to get a baseline of who is still
with you. Give away a prize or ask a trivia question to reset
the room.

- **They ask questions or comments of any kind.** All feedback is
  good. Even if it's to tell you how much you suck, it means
  they cared enough to fill out the form or write you an email.
  Any effort expended to respond to you, be it criticism, questions, suggestions, or references, is an indication you chose the
  right topic and held enough attention to generate a response.
  If they give advice or correct something, thank them, even if
  you disagree. It's a sign of respect that someone in your audience invested any energy in you at all.

- **The hosts invite you back.** The organizer's feedback is sometimes different from the audience's, but the rule of thumb is if
  you get invited back, you did better than most of the other
  people who spoke at the event.

# What to do when things go wrong

Since all public speaking is a kind of performance, things can and will go wrong, no matter how good you are. This list comes from my own experiences, as well as conversations with other veteran speakers. It's a handy reference for minimizing fears you might have, or for diagnosing how you could've done something differently after it happened.

## You're being heckled

Hecklers are rare. When it happens, the audience is usually as frustrated with him you are. Use this to your advantage. If you engage a heckler, you often look mean, but if you get the audience on your side, things end quickly.

Hecklers are people who wish they were on stage, are drunk, or think they are helping you by contributing.

**How to prevent:**

- Set the rules for how the audience can interact with you. If you want questions held until the end, say so; or, if you're OK with them at any time, let the audience know. Also set boundaries for Twitter and event chat rooms. I always give out my email address so everyone in the room has an outlet to say things they're not sure are appropriate during the lecture.

**How to respond:**

- Always remember you have more power than any heckler. If you have the microphone, you are amplified; he is not. You can interrupt or talk over him, and he can do nothing to stop you. It's really not a fair fight in any sense. As soon as a heckler realizes this, he will silence himself.

- Address whoever spoke and ask him to hold his comments or questions until the end. Done politely and calmly, this nearly always works. It shows you won't be rattled and that you'll stop the problem before it gets out of hand. Even if someone makes a joke at your expense, don't make it into an argument; politely ask him to wait until your presentation is over.

- If you are confident, you can quickly dispatch a heckler with a joke or funny comment—but be careful. If you're not good at this, you're entering a battle you might lose. It's easier to laugh at the joke, even if it's at your expense. Say, "That's interesting, thank you" but continue with your point. This gives him some respect, as you're acknowledging his voice, but keeps you in control.

- If someone is clearly out of line and upsetting other people, ask the event host to help. If the crowd is hostile or behaving inappropriately, the host should be willing to take action. You can ask the heckler to leave if he can't respect your rules, and the host should help make this happen if it's necessary.

## Everyone is staring at their laptops

Every audience has a culture, and in some cultures it's common for people to stare at something other than the speaker. This often takes energy away from the speaker, so it's usually to the speaker's advantage to have as much eye contact from the audience as possible. Sometimes people are just taking notes or sharing what you say with other people, which is good for you, but other times they're playing Solitaire or wandering the Web, which isn't good. People in the audience should be free to choose how they want to listen, but you are also free to influence how they make that choice.

**How to prevent:**

- You can ask people to close their laptops. Don't demand it—respect their right to do what they like, especially if they are paying to be in the room. But you can tell them you think you'll do a better job if you have the room's undivided attention.

- Sometimes I say the following: "Here's a deal. I'd like you to give me your undivided attention for five minutes. If after five minutes you're bored, you think I'm an idiot, or you'd rather browse the Web than listen, you're free to do so. In fact, I won't mind if you get up and leave after five minutes. But for the first 300 seconds, please give me your undivided attention." Most people close their laptops.

- Keep in mind that some people take notes on their laptops. They might be live blogging or tweeting what you're saying, vastly increasing your audience beyond the room. An open laptop doesn't always mean you're being ignored.

**How to respond:**

- There isn't much you can do, but you should focus on the people who are fully engaged.

- Go with the flow. Have Twitter open on your laptop, project it on the screen, and take a moment midway through your talk to review comments and questions.

- Ask the host to monitor Twitter or the event chat room as a way to get the best questions and comments from the back channel into your presentation. Let the audience know this is happening and how they can send a question to the host.

# Your time slot gets cut from 45 minutes to 10

Event schedules have mistakes, and speakers pay the price. Cancellations, travel delays, or other logistical problems put event organizers in difficult spots where they have no other choice but to limit your time. If your slot is late in the day, you may be forced to give a shorter presentation to make up the time.

**How to prevent:**

- Unless you're the organizer, it's not your job to keep others on time. If you do notice the schedule getting behind and your talk is late in the day, let the organizers know. Recommend they cut a break short, or ask several speakers to make up a few minutes each rather than force you to pick up the slack for the entire day.

**How to respond:**

- If your talk needs to be cut short, ask the organizer to introduce you and to tell the audience it's not your fault the schedule has fallen behind. This will at least get you some additional sympathy from the crowd.

## Everyone in the room hates you

There are days when the vibe in the room is all wrong, and it feels like the audience either hates you or just wants you to shut up. It can especially feel this way when speaking in foreign countries or in corporations that have just announced major layoffs (but no one told you this before). Or, maybe you actually did something stupid, and they rightfully hate you for it.

**How to prevent:**

- Your host is your guide. He should tell you if there is something you need to know, like recent layoffs or other bad news that might be on people's minds. If you're paranoid, you can ask, "Is there anything that happened recently I should know about?"
- Get there early. If you are early, you can introduce yourself and talk to people who will be in your audience. You'll get a feel for what they're like; it may change how you approach the larger group.

**How to respond:**

- On some days you just have to go into robotic mode, and give your presentation as if you are speaking to a crowd who likes you. Just do your thing and don't worry about the audience. If they hate you, they hate you, but don't fall into the trap of trying to change your presentation on the fly out of fear that they don't like you. It's impossible to do. Go on with the show enthusiastically for the sake of the handful of people who might hate you less than you think.

- Cut material to get to your Q&A quickly. If you have optional stories you sometimes tell, drop them. The sooner you get to Q&A, the faster you can diagnose what's going on. And at worst, the sooner your talk will be over.

## One guy won't stop asking questions

This is the polite variant of the heckler, and it's much more common. Some people don't realize they are abusing their question-asking privileges and fail to notice they are speaking almost as much as you are. Just be glad you're not married to someone like this—you'd never get a chance to speak at all.

In some cases, these people answer questions addressed to you because their drive to impress you, and others, is so strong.

**How to prevent:**

- The general rule is that people raise their hands with questions, and you pick who gets to speak. If you keep calling on the same person, whose fault is it?
- If people are yelling out questions or comments, ask them to first raise their hands.

**How to respond:**

- Realize the audience hates these people. They're annoying and often come off as teacher's pets, which no one likes. The sooner you quiet them down, the happier the audience will be with you.
- Just because a question is asked does not mean you are obligated to answer. Ask the audience, "How many people are interested in this question?" If only a fraction of the audience raises their hands, tell the asker to come up afterward and you'll answer then.
- During a break, talk to the person in private. Thank him for his contributions, but ask him to hold off on asking more questions so others can have a chance to contribute. Give him your email as an alternative way to ask questions.

## There is a rambling question that makes no sense and takes three minutes to ask

A good warning sign of this is a question that has a 60-second preamble. Whoever is asking a question this long hasn't thought about it enough yet to even form a question.

**How to prevent:**

- This is tough. Warning people to avoid rambling questions tends to intimidate them from asking anything at all. It's much better to respond when and if it happens.

**How to respond:**

- Ask a clarifying question, "Do you mean X or Y?" Interrupt people if necessary. If they seem lost, ask them to rethink their question while you answer the next question. Then go back to them later. This is pushy, but if you do it with charm, the audience appreciates it.

- Realize the audience hates these people, too. They didn't come to the session to hear someone's rambling, poorly formed pseudo-question. If someone is 30 seconds into a question, and you think he's going nowhere, you're the only one in the room who can do anything about it.

- If you do cut him off, remind him of your email address and mention that longer questions are fine—just not in real time.

- Sometimes people want to make a point of their own, which is more than fine, provided it's short. Same advice as above applies in this case.

## You are asked an impossible question

There is nothing wrong with a tough question you can't answer. There is no law that says you as the speaker must know everything. If you are speaking on an interesting topic, of course there will be questions you can't answer. There were plenty of questions Einstein couldn't answer either. Even omnipotent speakers can't answer the question, "What is something you can ask omnipotent speakers that they can't answer?"

## How to prevent:

- The only solution is to have a talk so boring, or so obscure, that tough questions are impossible because the audience doesn't know what the hell your point was. Don't do this.

## How to respond:

- Learn to say three words: "I don't know." They are easy to say. You will not die instantly if you say them.

- Write down the question or ask someone to email it to you, and promise you'll post an answer to your blog.

- Offer the question to the audience. Maybe you're not the only one who can't answer the question. If no one in the audience knows, they seem at least as dumb as you do. And if someone does know, you've helped the person who asked the tough question get an answer, even if it's not from you.

# The microphone breaks

Often microphones only partially break. They have feedback or flitter in and out. This is incredibly distracting for an audience, and they will blame you for it. If after a couple of minutes the problem doesn't resolve itself, assume the microphone is broken.

## How to prevent:

- Pray to the gods of A/V equipment.
- Demand a sound check before your talk.
- Ask the A/V people where there are sound problems in the room.

## How to respond:

- Confirm with the audience they are hearing the same problems you are. Sometimes the problems are only heard at the front of the stage.

- Get the tech crew involved. This is why they are paid. As embarrassing as it is for you, if you get them to help, the audience will know it's not entirely your fault.

- In moderately sized rooms (100 people or less), the acoustics are often good enough for people to hear you without a mike if you project well. Step forward, and you might be able to get started while the tech crew fixes things.

- The best filler material is to ask people what they hope to learn. Or ask people who have been in their current job for fewer than five years to raise their hands. They will always be able to answer, and it gives you some useful background data.

- If it's a long session, take a break. People like breaks. Rather than force them to watch you struggle with the equipment, give the audience five minutes to get coffee or go to the restroom.

## Your laptop explodes

At every conference, there is always at least one person who has technical problems with his computer. Some events force you to use their lectern computer to help minimize problems, but with video codecs and font issues, this sometimes makes it worse. Mac or PC, all computers have issues, and every projector and video system has charming idiosyncrasies that the tech people who manage them are in denial of.

**How to prevent:**

- Use your own gear.

- PC laptops are more popular, and I'm convinced they have fewer issues with projector compatibility. Problem is, they're PCs.

- Demand a video check before your talk.

**How to respond:**

- The big question is when to abandon your laptop. Ten minutes is my cutoff point. If after 10, you're still not sure what to do, go with Plan B.

- Plan B: know your core points (see Chapter 5). Be able to write them down as a short bulleted list. Do a shorter, less formal version of your talk. Don't constantly say, "If I had my slides" or "In my real presentation...." The audience doesn't care about what they might have seen.

- Have a printout of your slides with you. Worst case, you can use this as your notes.

## There is a typo on your slide (nooooo!)

This one is easy. Who cares? Sure, it's nice to spell people's names right and to try to make things perfect for your audience, but mistakes will be made. The web, blog, and Twitter world has made everyone much more forgiving of bad spelling and punctuation. If a typo is your biggest mistake, you've done very well.

**How to prevent:**

- Have a friend flip through your slides.

**How to respond:**

- Thank whoever caught it and make a note to fix the mistake. Then move on.

## You're late for your own talk

For reasons explained in Chapter 3, this can happen easily if you are speaking somewhere new. Being late, honestly, happens when you don't plan to arrive early enough. You can make sure traffic, late flights, confusing directions, and all the things that cause delays don't kill you, provided you arrive hours early or the night before.

**How to prevent:**

- Get there early. Fly in the night before. Do not assume the travel world works perfectly because it never does.

**How to respond:**

- At the first moment you think you might be late, call your hosts. They may be able to swap your time slot with another speaker. The sooner they know, the more options they have, and the less they will hate you.

- When you do arrive, no matter how late you are, take a moment to reset yourself. If you are frantic and panicked, you can't possibly do a good job. It's worth being an extra 30 seconds late to make sure that you're calm for whatever time you have left to speak.

- Before you close, offer to stay late for anyone who has follow-up questions. It's a good habit anyway, but this might mitigate people's gripes about your late arrival.

## You feel sick

This is a judgment call because everyone handles being sick differently. Some people can manage a cold or a headache so well that if they don't mention it, no one would know. Other people can't concentrate at all.

**How to prevent:**

- If you know you're speaking the next day, don't go out drinking the night before.
- Eat an apple a day.

**How to respond:**

- The big question is whether you should cancel. This depends heavily on how easy it is to reschedule. Talk with your hosts as soon as you feel sick and let them tell you what the options are. Given the choice of seeing a half-baked lecture from a sick person or rescheduling to see a good lecture from a healthy person, most of the audience would prefer the latter. But if it's a one-shot deal, like at a conference or if they've all come just to hear you, they'd prefer the former.
- Always bring some aspirin with you. It won't cure your flu or cold, but it will make you feel better for a couple of hours, just enough time to get through a presentation.

## You're running out of time

This happens much more often than people ending early. Since most people practice to finish exactly on time, with little buffer, it's not a surprise.

**How to prevent:**

- If you build your presentation right, there should be a steady rhythm throughout the talk that informs you of your pace every step of the way (see Chapter 6). This prevents you from discovering you have one minute left to cover half of your talk.
- Practice to use less time than you are given.
- Plan to have 20–30% of your time slot for Q&A. If you run over, you can eat some of that Q&A time.

- Use a remote control that has a timer.

- Ask your host to warn you when there are 15 minutes remaining, or whatever is one-third of your total time.

**How to respond:**

- Don't get lost. If you can't get through the material, put it aside and focus on your audience. If you have three sections left and only time for one, let the audience vote on which section it should be.

- Quality is always more important than quantity. Don't cram or rush. Always be willing to abandon material so the material you have time for can be done well.

- Offer to provide the slides on your website for any material you did not get to.

- Offer to come back again to cover the remaining material and answer any follow-up questions people have.

## You left your slide deck at home

Hey, it happens. Perhaps you copied them to the wrong place or left your flash drive in the airport restroom.

**How to prevent:**

- Put your slides in three places: on a flash drive you bring with you, on your own laptop, and on a website you can access from any web browser. Redundancy wins.

- For the paranoid, print out a copy as well. Sometimes analog beats digital—if the power goes out and you have a flashlight, you'll be all set.

**How to respond:**

- The gutsy way to go is to admit it to the audience. Apologize. Beg their forgiveness and improvise a way to be useful to them anyway.

- The simple trick is to make a list of 10 questions at the start of your talk, pulled live from the audience, and answer each question in turn. What do they expect to learn? This may turn out to be much better material than what you had planned.

## Your hosts are control freaks

Sometimes the people who host you ask—or are told by their bosses to demand—all kinds of annoying things. This can include using ugly slide templates, instructing you not to say certain things or tell certain stories, and most often, wanting you to sign waivers that give them the right to videotape and photograph you for use of their own choosing.

As the speaker, you are providing a service. You can refuse or ask to strike out conditions you don't like.

**How to prevent:**

- You can let organizers know you don't like being videotaped, or set other conditions, early on. Professional speakers often have info sheets they give prospective venues that list their requirements or things they won't do.

**How to respond:**

- Politely explain why the condition works against your goals. If videotaping makes you nervous, regardless of why, explain that videotaping will reduce the satisfaction of people actually in the audience.

- Slide templates are stupid 95% of the time. They're meant to improve slide quality, but they're always based on Power-Point templates, which are notoriously bad, bullet heavy, and ugly. A decent compromise is to use the title slide from their template but nothing else. Never let them auto-update your slides based on a template, as it always messes up layouts and complex slides in evil ways event organizers will rarely notice.

- Simply strike out the offending clauses, initial them, and return the contract, mentioning what you did. This is often perfectly acceptable.

- If they insist on video or audio recording, demand a Creative Commons license so you can reuse that recording yourself. This will allow them to do what they wish with the recording, but also gives you the right to post the video on your website or to YouTube, or to sell it. It's quite fair to ask for this: you get a professional recording you can reuse, and they get the right to film you at all.

## You have a wardrobe malfunction

This happens to people performing at the Super Bowl all the time. And even for people less famous than Janet Jackson, many unfortunate things can happen to clothing over lunch or in a public restroom.

**How to prevent:**

- Have the host or a friend in the audience look you over before you begin.
- Remove all nipple piercings well before your lecture begins.
- Always make a pass through the restroom before you go on and check yourself in the mirror. A good time is right before they want to put a microphone on you and after you've made sure your laptop and other tech gear are working properly. Check your teeth (spinach is evil) and your fly, and talk at the mirror and move around just to see if anything silly is going on.
- One plus to being early on the schedule is that the odds of spilling something on yourself go way down.

**How to respond:**

- If you notice something you can fix discreetly, hide behind the lectern to do it. The lectern covers many sins.
- Bring a sweater or extra shirt just in case something bad happens. A sweater can be put on over your shirt or wrapped around your waist, covering whatever it is you wish to hide.
- And of course, find a way not to care about superficial things you can't change. Make a joke or tell a story of a worse experience, but above all, don't let yourself be upstaged by a stain, a rip, or an open zipper.

## There are only five people in the audience

There is a magic number when the audience is so small that it's no longer an audience but more of a group. The mistake is to pretend it's still a big crowd and to give a fancy presentation designed for a large audience. It won't work. You have to switch gears.

**How to prevent:**

- Have a sign-up sheet for your talk. Most conferences do this by default. You should always know how many are registered. Drop-off rates for lectures are high, usually around 50%. If 100 people sign up, you should expect 50 to attend.

- Do some research. How many people showed up to the last lecture that took place at this venue? Are there good reasons to assume your material will draw a larger crowd?

- Promote yourself. Two things have to happen to have a big crowd: interested people need to be made aware of your talk, and then they need incentive to come.

**How to respond:**

- Use the density theory. If you're in a big room, get everyone together. If it's really only five people, make a nice semicircle so a conversation is natural.

- Drop your prepared slide deck. Odds are slim that it will go over well with a small group. Switch to informal mode, and start the session by making a list of questions as described previously in "You left your slide deck at home." Then answer them.

## What to do if your situation is not here

Well, my friend, there is only one fail-safe maneuver. You must pay attention to what happens so you can tell your friends about it later. As you'll see next, true disasters always make for great stories you can share with other people.

# You can't do worse than this

We all have great stories we tell our friends about something in life gone horribly wrong. Bad things happen. Life goes on. And eventually what was miserable becomes funny, at least for our friends. These stories work because they make others feel better about things going wrong in their lives, including the person it happened to.

I've compiled this list for that single reason: to make everyone feel better. Whatever you're afraid of, I suspect it's not anywhere near as bad as what happened to these folks. And these are all smart, experienced speakers. It's an honor to make the list, and I'm grateful to all the people who contributed a story.

## Does anyone speak Georgian?

My worst was also one of my first. I was asked to "attend" a conference of "senior government officials" in Georgia (as in the Republic of). I arrived late in the evening and was taken to a government house to sleep. The driver woke me at 7 a.m., and we left at 7:30 to drive an hour or so to a government office. When I arrived, I found about 50 top officials, from the president of the Supreme Court (and most of the Court), to the leaders of the parliament, and about 20 representatives from the president's office. I was seated at the head of the table. No translator for me. The president of the Court began—two sentences in English welcoming me, and then 20 minutes or so to the audience in Georgian.

He then turned to me and said in English, "Now, we'd like you to give a one-hour talk comparing the German, French, and American constitutions, with any special insight for Georgia."

I know, you've had that dream. But this was for real.

—Lawrence Lessig
*Professor of Law,*
*Stanford Law School*

## What to do when the SWAT team comes

Moscow, 1997. I was one of several speakers at a consumer electronics company–sponsored "thank you" dinner in a magnificent restaurant. Several important executives had flown in from Tokyo for the evening.

Thirty seconds into my talk, the doors burst open and six balaclava-hooded and heavily armed OMON troops (Moscow equivalent of a SWAT team) moved into the room. They did not speak. Neither did I.

Four of them occupied the corners of the room while two headed directly for a table on the far side, AK-47s drawn. They grabbed a man at the table, stood him up, and marched him out of the dining room. All quiet, the remaining four sidled out.

I finished my talk. The Tokyo executives never returned to Moscow.

—Dan Roam
*author of* The Back of the
Napkin *(Portfolio)*

## A funny thing happened on my way to the stage

After a long night of conference partying many years ago, I overslept and woke up only moments before I was supposed to give a talk. Not only did I have a killer hangover, I was fairly certain that I was still drunk. I raced out of the hotel room in which I had fallen asleep, horrified to realize that, at some point during the night's adventures, I had swapped my shirt for a new T-shirt that read, "I fuck like a girl." Given how late I was and how far away from my own hotel, I had to go as-is. Before entering the conference hall, I decided that I needed a cigarette. I walked up to a cute girl who was happy to offer me one. Yet, after I took a deep inhale, I quickly realized that it wasn't filled with tobacco.

Somehow, I still managed to give my talk. Luckily, this was SXSW, a conference jokingly called spring break for geeks, and many in attendance were wearing sunglasses to cover their own remnants of the night before.

—danah boyd
*Social media blogger*

## Death by lecture

One of the few stories of a lecture killing someone comes straight from the Bible.

"Seated in a window was a young man named Eutychus, who was sinking into a deep sleep as Paul talked on and on. When he was sound asleep, he fell to the ground from the third story and was picked up dead. Paul went down, threw himself on the young man and put his arms around him."

*from Acts 20:9–12*

## CEO demo gone wrong

While working at Microsoft, I flew all the way to Toronto to do a demo during Steve Ballmer's keynote for COMDEX Canada. The whole demo was supposed to be five minutes. I walked on stage, clicked one button, the demo machine started flashing and having a seizure, and 15 seconds later I was headed off stage.

All that time and money spent for 45 seconds of public humiliation. And of course, the picture on the front of the Toronto paper the next day was of me and Ballmer laughing uncomfortably while I was flailing. I'm sure he loved that the press decided that my 45 seconds were the most important part of his keynote.

—Hillel Cooperman
*www.jacksonfish.com*

## Do not set anything on fire

Twenty-five-year-old Leonard Susskind was asked to give a talk at the Institute for Advanced Study at Princeton University. In the front row were J. Robert Oppenheimer, Nobel Laureate T. D. Lee, and many other notables. Susskind was young and terrified, and responded by being overly aggressive and defensive. It was 1965, and at that time they used opaque projectors, which were sandwiched between glass and projected by a bright light on a screen. Famous physicist Marvin Goldberg asked a question, and in trying to answer, Susskind got his red tie stuck in the projector he was using to give the presentation, and it burst into flames. Goldberg stood up, grabbed a glass of water, and splashed Susskind in the face to put it out.[1]

## No one likes surprise porn

Back around 2004, I was running a presentation to the newly formed New Zealand Chapter of the Usability Professionals' Association. The room was full of geeks, web managers, consultants, and librarian-types.

To introduce new and potential members to the organization, I opened a web browser to call up the website and proceeded to type *http://www.upass.org*.

Unsavory things being done to butts flashed up on screen, followed by gasps and laughter, some fainting, and one "Yahoo!" A quick Alt+F4 came in handy. Since then, all my presentations have had very high turnouts, although a significant portion of the audience wears dark shades.

The proper URL was *http://www.upassoc.org*.

—Zef
*http://www.zefmedia.com*

## I see sleeping people

Early last year, I was presenting at a user group. Partway through the presentation, I noticed some of them giggling. One of them even left the room briefly to regain composure. Fearing that it was something about the way I was presenting, I started rushing things and having mental blanks partway through sentences (hoping I wasn't *that* boring). In between the muffled giggling, I heard this deep, nasal breathing. Looking toward the source, I discovered an older guy was actually asleep! I remarked, "Oh, we've got a sleeper." With that, the room erupted in laughter, waking the poor guy up. He left the session embarrassed.

---

[1] Leonard Susskind tells the full version of this story at a lecture at Stanford University, February 2, 2005. You can watch it here: *http://tinyurl.com/susskind*.

I felt really awkward about that whole presentation. I just hope to God that the video isn't lurking somewhere on the Internet.

—Daniel

## At worst we will shoot you

I'm afraid many of my best stories are classified. But the gist is the same: presenting at any kind of high-security facility is infallibly a nightmare. Does your laptop have (a) WiFi, or (b) Bluetooth, or (c) an integrated camera, or (d) a microphone, or (e) a USB port (into which thumb drives may be inserted), or (f) an Ethernet or Firewire port, or (g) a PC card slot, or…etc. If so, then it's not coming through our door. Basically, if it's not a pure output device, we can't admit it. And no, you can't bring the presentation in on a thumb drive. Mail us a PDF of the slides, which we'll "wash," install on a secure server, then our technician will run them for you from a locked room somewhere else in the building. Oh, and never leave the direct line-of-sight of your designated escort, because then (at best) it's a rubber glove search for you. And at worst? We might mistakenly shoot you.

—Damian Conway
*author of* Perl Best Practices
*(O'Reilly)*

## Don't blame the trains

Years ago I was a freelancer, hired to do talks and courses about Microsoft Office technologies and programming. One morning, I was traveling by train to start with a new group, and all circumstances were against me. The Dutch railway system fucked up my schedule with so many ridiculous problems, I couldn't keep count. So I arrived half an hour too late, and apologized for my lateness.

I then tried to repair my damaged image by making lots of jokes and complaints about the Dutch railway system. (I thought that if there's one thing that unites an audience, it's the sharing of pain.)

Unfortunately, it turned out that this particular group was working for, and sent by, the Dutch railway company. My reputation with them never recovered.

—Jurgen Appelo
*www.noop.nl*

## You work where?

In 1997, after I'd been working at the highly influential Hot-Wired website for a year or so, I went back to my alma matter to give a talk to a web design class about working in the nascent web industry.

I stood in front of the class and told what I thought were highly entertaining stories about life at HotWired for a half-hour. When I finally stopped and asked if anyone had questions, one hand meekly raised in the back.

The question was, "What's HotWired?"

—Derek Powazek
*http://powazek.com*

## Watch your slides

I was traveling to FOSDEM in February 2006 on the Eurostar from London. I was due to give the opening presentation in the Mozilla room on the state of the Mozilla Foundation. The Foundation/Corporation split had happened in mid-2005, so people were eager to hear what the future held.

I arrived at Brussels Midi and decided to save a quid or two of the Foundation's money by taking the subway rather than a taxi. I went down into the subway station and tried to buy a ticket. The ticket machine utterly baffled me. After five minutes of trying, I turned round in frustration to find that my wheeled luggage had been stolen. I had lost everything except, praise God, my pass-port, wallet, and return ticket, which were in my jacket pockets. But my suitcase, clothes, and laptop—with my presentation for Saturday—were all gone.

Fortunately, I arrived early enough that I had time to go clothes shopping. But the 45-minute talk had to happen from memory. These days, I always take a cab to the hotel.

—Gerv Markham
*www.gerv.net*

## Why you don't want to be up against Bono

For my first major speaking engagement, I was to speak at COMDEX on "Building Large-Scale e-Commerce Systems."

This was during the first boom, before Amazon was #1, when scale was *very* hard. We'd done it, and folks wanted to hear about it.

I was flown to Chicago to give a 90-minute talk in a room that could hold 1,200 people. It was empty, so I set up. As the time to speak approached, I wasn't sure why the room wasn't filling up. I walked around, checked the signage, confirmed the room number and time. There was just a smattering of people in the room. I figured I could start late if something had happened.

The time to start came and went...five people in a room to hold 1,200! Was I going insane? I could hear the crowd outside— COMDEX *was* packed that year. I went into the hall, toward the din, and saw him. Linus Torvalds (founder of Linux). Speaking in the room across from the room I was speaking in. That room had standing-room only, overflowing into the hallway.

I returned to my own 1,200-seat room, sat on the edge of the stage, and delivered my talk to five attendees.

—Scott Hanselman
*www.hanselman.com*

## You will never speak of this to anyone

Standing up in front of 30 bright-eyed high school seniors the first day back to school from the Christmas holidays in 1983 will stand in my mind for all eternity. We used "chalk" back then, and I was at the chalkboard doing one of my brilliant presentations about vector analysis (I think I was as bored as my students) when I dropped the chalk. I bent over to pick it up, and guess what? In short, I farted in class. It was not an SBD (silent but deadly) but a real rip-roarer. I don't really know where it came from. I stood up and turned to the class to see the astonished faces staring at me in disbelief. All I could think to say was, "Excuse me." Then we all cracked up. I threatened them with every inch of their lives and told them I would fail anyone who uttered a word of this to the outside. Yeah, it made the school paper the next week. Took me the rest of the semester to live that down. When Facebook came out, I hooked up with a bunch of my old students to see how they turned out. Yep, they all reminded me of the incident. I think it was permanently engraved on their brains forever.

—Martin Yarborough
*www.mpttech.com/blog*

# Watch where you sit

In 1996, I was giving my first-ever conference presentation at a workshop about quantum information held at the Santa Fe Institute in New Mexico. I was 22 years old and very nervous, since the audience contained many quantum information big shots. The talk went well, and I got to the end. The audience clapped, and the Chair started to suggest that we should break for lunch.

I say *started* because he didn't complete what he was saying. The spotlight of attention having moved elsewhere, I decided to relax. Unfortunately, I did this by starting to seat myself on the "table" that had supported the overhead projector during my talk.

I say "table" because it looked superficially like a table, but it actually didn't have four legs for support. In fact, it was supported on a single pillar, so nothing supported the edges. I sat down on an edge, and the entire table collapsed, catapulting the projector all the way over my body, now lying prone on the floor.

—Martin Nielsen

# Please make a new talk and give it five minutes from now

In February 2002, I was invited to TED to talk about Project Orion (the post-Sputnik pre-NASA interplanetary space vehicle). At TED, everyone gets 18 minutes on stage—no exceptions. I had 18 minutes of slides all set. The conference closely followed 9/11, and all eyes were on the invasion of Taliban-controlled Afghanistan. At the last minute—and I mean last minute—Chris Anderson, who was just taking the helm of TED, managed to secure Zohra Yousuf Daoud, the first (and so far only) Miss Afghanistan, as a speaker. Could I cut my time to eight minutes? I guess so! No time to edit my slides, so I divided 80 into 480 seconds and set them on 6-second auto-advance, climbed on stage, and tried to keep up. Finished right on time, but I don't remember anything else.

—George Dyson
*author of* Project Orion *(Holt)*[2]

---

[2] You can watch this talk here: *http://www.ted.com/talks/george_dyson_on_project_orion.html*.

## Check your mirror

Last year, I had a morning speaking engagement in Florida. Always the prepared flyer, I planned my flight for the day before. One hurricane-level winds in Houston warning, a stopover in Cleveland, a layover in Nashville, and 24 hours later, I landed in Orlando. On the bright side, I only travel with carry-on luggage. My computer, clothes, and everything I needed were right there with me. On the downside, I realized somewhere between Nashville and Orlando that I would be arriving with minutes to spare, and I was in my jeans-and-T-shirt travel outfit.

With the help of a sympathetic stewardess, I did my hair and makeup, then I changed into my suit, using every yoga position imaginable within that tiny airplane bathroom.

My cab got me from the airport to the convention center with 10 minutes to spare. I made it onstage, gathered myself, and walked out with a smile. I made it through the hour, and wrapped up the presentation (a training for the IT-challenged about online software) with a line I used often:

"You see, you don't have to be a techie to understand even the more complicated programs, you just have to know how to explore."

Then an audience member piped up, "No, but it helps if you're a Trekkie!"

I noticed the sound guy trying not to fall over laughing offstage. He pointed to me, then pointed to his chest.

I glanced at the video screen behind me to discover that the shirt I had hastily dressed over was clearly showing off its main graphic—a yellow and black Star Trek communicator—right through my blouse.

—Cassandra

## Waterproofing cannot save you

At TED I did a live, and unfortunately, unrehearsed demo of the Nanotex waterproof khakis. I took a glass of water and splashed my waist with vigor to show how it would leave no mark. In a freak instance of fabric folding, the bolus of water hooked into a gaping open pant pocket. The inner pocket lining did not have any

Nanotex coating.... So, for the entire talk my boxers were soaking wet, but you wouldn't know it because none of the water could seep through the outer pants fabric.

—Steve Jurvetson
*Managing Director,*
*Draper Fisher Jurvetson*

## Why you should not lecture in bars

My flight arrived into Boston, Massachusetts, at 5:05 p.m., and I needed to be at Tommy Doyle's bar in Cambridge for a 7 p.m. keynote. I planned to take the subway, but it turned out the Silver line from the airport was actually just a twice-an-hour van driven by an idiot. I arrived at the bar at 6:59 p.m. The place was packed, but packed with people who had been drinking since happy hour while waiting for the event, Ignite! Boston, to begin. At 7:02 p.m., I learned the only laptop I could use was a Mac, a Mac that completely rejected my remote control. I was forced to stand on stage, with someone else's laptop on a bar stool, and manually click through my slides.

The bar was long with my small stage at the far, short end, creating a wind tunnel of bad acoustics. Not only could I not hear myself well, but the long, tunnel shape of the bar channeled all the noise from the large crowd of people drinking in the back up and over the much smaller crowd trying to listen. This made everyone unhappy and not so interested in listening to me. In response, much of the crowd, even those up front, were having their own conversations, often commenting to one another about what I was saying as I said it. Just minutes in, struggling to feel in control of the room, I was heckled by a woman when I mentioned Crick and Watson discovered DNA, without recognizing the often-overlooked Rosalind Franklin. I had enough and was pissed off. I made a joke about how now we know where the feminists in the crowd are. A joke that received mostly boos. It was all downhill from there. I finished as quickly as I could. I made a beeline for the bar, downing beers and shots of vodka, trying to forget what happened.

Hours later, Ignite! nearly over and me finally in a proper drunken stupor, the organizers found me. They wanted me to speak *again*.

To the same hostile crowd in the same awful room as the dreaded unannounced closing speaker. I did something I would never do again: I said yes. They were friends who seemed desperate, and I was shitfaced, so how could I say no? I got up on stage, grabbed the microphone, and extemporaneously talked about...I don't remember what I said. Which is probably the best for all involved.

—Scott Berkun
*Public speaker*

# Research and recommendations

If you want to know what sources beyond life experience shaped my opinions, or want advice on what to read next, this is for you.

There are two bibliographies—one annotated, the other ranked—and a summary of other research used to support the writing of this book.

## Annotated bibliography

### How to get over fears and anxiety

The best advice is to seek out your local Toastmasters group. It's run and organized by supportive people interested in helping you. There are thousands of local groups, so visit *http://www. toastmasters.org* to find your local chapter.

Karen Kangas Dwyer's book *Conquer Your Speech Anxiety* (Wadsworth), picked up cheap at a used bookstore, changed my thinking about fear. Unlike other good books on the subject, such as *The Francis Effect*, by M. F. Fensholt (Oakmont Press), this is a workbook. Along with each chapter are exercises designed to help you understand your unique set of fears, and to accept and work through them. It comes with a CD that helps with the exercises.

### How to tell great stories

One chapter that didn't make it into the book was about story-telling and how it's the foundation of all good speaking and writing. I chose instead to do it rather than merely write about doing it, and I hope you found the stories in this book effective and memorable.

Anthony Bourdain's *Kitchen Confidential* (Harper Perennial) and George Orwell's *Down and Out in Paris and London* (Mariner Books) were major inspirations for many reasons, especially in choosing to use my own stories as the central theme of the book (also see William Zinsser's *Inventing the Truth* [Mariner Books]). I'm convinced well-written, honest, first-person narrative has powers to connect and teach, which stuffy third-person writing never can. It might be hard to believe here at the end of this book, but my faith in first person, and not egotism, motivated the choice to center the book on myself as the main character. It is strange to me that so many photos of myself are in the book, but it was driven by the goal of effectively telling stories, which happened to be mostly my own. If you thought my stories sucked, or were annoyed by all the photos, at least here in the depths of the bibliography you're safe from any further disappointments.

The best advice on becoming a better storyteller is to dive head first into listening to great stories, which is easier than ever to do today. Start with NPR's *This American Life* (*www.thisamericanlife.org*), a weekly one-hour show that weaves three or more stories on a theme into captivating, entertaining, and intimate storytelling. Some of these shows completely floor me and make me wonder why this stuff isn't more popular. You will not hear statistics, data, or any analytical bullshit we pretend to care about, yet somehow these stories move, convince, and emote without them. Why? You'll have to listen to find out.

If *TAL*'s format is too long, or you don't like the host Ira Glass (who I love, but some don't), check out *The Moth* (*www.themoth.org*), a series of 10- to 15-minute stories told without notes in front of live audiences. And there is also *StoryCorps* (*www.storycorps.org*), which captures its stories on the streets of American cities. All are available free online and in podcast form. Highly recommended. If *This American Life*, *The Moth*, or *StoryCorps* don't move you in some way, see a doctor immediately—you might be dead.

*The Story Factor*, by Annette Simmons (Perseus Books Group), is an exceptional book. It illustrates how we use stories all the time in everyday life and provides clear guidance on how to get better at telling stories and using them more effectively in life and work situations.

## How to teach

Teaching is a skill, and the best way to improve is to find someone who wants to learn something you know. You'll discover more from actually teaching than reading about it, and what you do read in books will only make sense if you have some teaching experiences of your own—however informal—to compare them with.

Teaching in America has problems, but rarely are they as well classified and solved as they are in Ken Bain's short book, *What the Best College Teachers Do* (Harvard University Press). Somehow we forget all of our college professors' teaching flaws after we graduate, assuming what we experienced is the only way it's done. Bain provides evidence that there are other ways, and he points to professors who do more than repeat the same boring lectures year after year.

An interesting exercise I performed while researching this book was to ask everyone I could find who their best teachers were and why. The answers consistently lined up with what Bain offers, but hearing it firsthand from so many people confirmed for me the advice in Bain's book.

## Presentation design

I avoided talking about presentation design in this book in part because it's a subject that has been covered well by others. Garr Reynolds's *Presentation Zen* (New Riders) and Nancy Duarte's *Slide:ology* (O'Reilly) are both solid sources for rethinking how you build your presentations. Both books offer many examples from experienced speakers as to how they put together actual slides for talks.

I'm particularly enamored with Reynolds's recommendation to work on paper until you figure out what you want to say and how you might say it. Starting with presentation software nearly always makes you think slide-centric and not story-, point-, or audience-centric.

## Studying comedians

Go back and listen to your favorite stand-up comedians do their long routines. They have all of the challenges speakers have, plus the burden of working without slides in front of intoxicated, paying audiences who demand not only that they make sense, but that they're funny, too. Many of the little tricks I've learned as a speaker come from listening to comedians—the master speakers of our age. Richard Pryor, Steve Martin, Henry Rollins, George Carlin, and Chris Rock are all exceptional and diverse profiles in how to communicate complex ideas effectively to crowds. They often take on surprisingly serious issues like politics, race relations, psychology, and war—issues most of us are afraid to discuss openly. They pull it off in part because they offer potent insights while making us laugh. Simply ask yourself, "How would <insert comedian here> give this presentation I'm supposed to give next week?", and you'll be forced to think more critically about how you might present the material. Of course, don't actually present it like <insert comedian here> unless you're either amazingly good or you want to find out exactly how the unemployment system works.

The documentary film *Comedian*, starring Jerry Seinfeld, is perhaps the best 90 minutes any frequent public speaker can spend in understanding how much effort is required to seem as effortless as good comedians seem. Even if you don't like Jerry Seinfeld's humor, you'll also hear from Chris Rock, Colin Quinn, Bill Cosby, and various other well-known comedians on how they prepare, find material, and perform. The focus of the film is on the year Seinfeld abandoned all his old material, and how he went about creating, practicing, and developing the new material—through many less than spectacular gigs—into an entirely new live show.

## How to make a living as a public speaker

There are many books that claim to teach you how to make $100,000 or $1,000,000 annually as a speaker. I'm convinced that stockpiling of wealth isn't the best use of these skills, as thinking and communicating better will help every important relationship you have, including your own relationship with yourself.

If you are driven by wages, few of these books explain, as I did in Chapter 3, that fame or expertise drives most speaking engagements, and without it you can be the best public speaker of all time and most of the world won't care. Having subject-matter expertise makes getting paid to speak possible. There are various certificates and degrees in public speaking, but if you look at the top 500 speakers in the world, I bet almost none of them have these credentials. If you have expertise in a subject, you can find organizations that run conferences and training events on that subject, and they often hire people to give lectures and teach seminars at their events. You will likely need, as I did, to do this for free for years until your skills and reputation provide demonstrable value.

Alan Weiss's *Money Talks: How to Make a Million As a Speaker* (McGraw-Hill) was the best professional reference I found for how to make a living as a public speaker. It's the book with the least fluff, and it has the most honest—often brutally so—breakdown on how to find people who will hire you, the value proposition from their point of view, and how to use all this to your advantage.

## Ranked bibliography

Traditional bibliographies provide little value. They obscure the relative value of prior works, and fail to indicate how the author used them (devoured, skimmed, or as a paperweight?). In addition to the preceding annotated bibliography, I experimented with different formats for a comprehensive listing—the result is this ranked bibliography. The intention is to indicate which sources drew attention during my research.

The order below is based on a review of over 150 pages of my research notes, from over 50 books. Every note I took from a book during research counted as one point, and the references are listed in ranked order. There are other books referenced in the text that may not appear here, as they served to support or reference a specific point rather than as an overall contribution to my thinking. There is no ideal system for ranking influence (the flaw in this one is that not all notes influenced me equally, and some good books didn't score any notes at all), but this was the best of all those suggested.

40, *What's the Use of Lectures?*, Donald A. Bligh (Jossey-Bass)

31, *Speak Like Churchill, Stand Like Lincoln: 21 Powerful Secrets of History's Greatest Speakers*, James C. Humes (Three Rivers Press)

28, *Public Speaking for Success*, Dale Carnegie (Tarcher)

28, *Lend Me Your Ears: All You Need to Know About Making Speeches and Presentations*, Max Atkinson (Oxford University Press)

26, *Brain Rules: 12 Principles for Surviving and Thriving at Work, Home, and School*, John Medina (Pear Press)

26, *History of Public Speaking in America*, Robert T. Oliver (Allyn & Bacon)

25, *Money Talks: How to Make a Million As a Speaker*, Alan Weiss (McGraw-Hill)

23, *Um: Slips, Stumbles, and Verbal Blunders, and What They Mean*, Michael Erard (Anchor)

22, *Conquer Your Speech Anxiety*, Karen Kangas Dwyer (Wadsworth)

22, *The Francis Effect: The Real Reason You Hate Public Speaking and How to Get Over It*, M. F. Fensholt (Oakmont Press)

20, *What the Best College Teachers Do*, Ken Bain (Harvard University Press)

15, *The Lost Art of the Great Speech: How to Write One—How to Deliver It*, Richard Dowis (AMACOM)

14, *Speak for a Living: The Insider's Guide to Building a Profitable Speaking Career*, Anne Bruce (ASTD Press)

13, *How People Learn*, National Research Council (National Academies Press)

12, *Secrets of Successful Speakers: How You Can Motivate, Captivate, and Persuade*, Lilly Walters (McGraw-Hill)

12, *Give Your Speech, Change the World: How to Move Your Audience to Action*, Nick Morgan (Harvard Business Press)

11, *Mastery: The Keys to Success and Long-Term Fulfillment*, George Leonard (Plume)

10, *I Can See You Naked*, Ron Hoff (Andrews McMeel Publishing)

10, *Confessions of a White House Ghostwriter*, James C. Humes (Regnery Publishing, Inc.)

10, *Thank You for Arguing*, Jay Heinrichs (Three Rivers Press)

8, *Yes! 50 Scientifically Proven Ways to Be Persuasive*, Noah J. Goldstein, Steve J. Martin, and Robert B. Cialdini (Free Press)

6, *Inventing the Truth: The Art and Craft of Memoir*, William Zinsser (Mariner Books)

5, *Presentation Zen: Simple Ideas on Presentation Design and Delivery*, Garr Reynolds (New Riders)

4, *Slide:ology: The Art and Science of Creating Great Presentations*, Nancy Duarte (O'Reilly)

4, *Made to Stick: Why Some Ideas Survive and Others Die*, Chip Heath and Dan Heath (Random House)

3, *Smart Speaking: 60-Second Strategies for More Than 100 Speaking Problems and Fears*, Laurie Schloff and Marcia Yudkin (Plume)

2, *The Years with Ross*, James Thurber (Harper Perennial)

2, *Speaking: From Intention to Articulation*, Willem J. M. Levelt (MIT Press)

2, *Pecha Kucha Night: 20 Images x 20 Seconds*, Klein Dytham Architecture (Klein Dytham)

1, *Better: A Surgeon's Notes on Performance*, Atul Gawande (Picador)

1, *Green Eggs and Ham*, Dr. Seuss (Random House Books for Young Readers)

## Other research sources

- **Interviews.** Over the course of two years, I interviewed more than 70 people, ranging from phone/email conversations to chats over dim sum. I talked to comedians, musicians, teachers, professors, trainers, and ordinary folks.

- **Lectures and discussion.** I presented some of the book's themes in lectures at Ignite! Seattle, Presentation Camp Seattle, and O'Reilly's FOO Camp.

- **Blog.** *www.speakerconfessions.com* served as a sounding board for some of the ideas in this book and was the primary source of the disaster stories. It also has some very good posts on aspects of public speaking that were not included in this book.

- **Survey.** Over 150 people who identified themselves as having presented in the O'Reilly Ignite! or Pecha Kucha format filled out an online questionnaire about their experiences preparing, presenting, and afterward. Results are posted on *www.speakerconfessions.com* (search for *ignite research*).

# How to help this book: a request

Thank you for buying this book. If it somehow exceeded your expectations or left you feeling like, gee, things would be better if more people read it, this is for you.

As you know by now, I'm a young, independent author. I don't have a huge marketing machine behind me, nor a gang of billionaire friends, or even a magic genie offering me three wishes. But that's OK. If you're willing to chip in a few minutes of your time, you can seriously help this book find its way in the cold, tough world, where many good books never reach all the people they should.

Please consider doing any of the following:

- Write a review on Amazon.com.
- Post about this book to your blog, on Facebook, or on Twitter.
- Recommend the book to coworkers, your friends and your friends' friends, or your friends with blogs, or your coworkers' friends who blog, or even your friends of friends who blog about their friends' blogs. The possibilities are endless.
- If you know people who write for newspapers or magazines, drop them a line, or perhaps Oprah or Jon Stewart owes you a favor. If so, now is a good time to cash it in.
- Check out *www.scottberkun.com* and discover all the great things I write about each week. If you like what you find, run through this list again with that in mind.

These little things make a huge difference. As the author, my opinion of the book carries surprisingly little weight. But you, dear reader, have all the power in the world.

Not only can you help this book find its way, but you'd also make the many risks of writing the next book easier to overcome, increasing the odds that I'll do an even better job next time around.

As always, thanks for your help and support.

# Acknowledgments

Special note: I owe the life that led to this book to people who buy my books, recommend my writings to others, leave comments on my blog, and help me get hired to speak at various places around the world. I'd be an idiot for not thanking you here. Thank you. You've changed my life and helped me chase my dreams, and I hope this book, or the next one, repays that debt. Your mere mentions of my work to others in person, on blogs, or wherever you do it makes my life possible. Please, pretty please, continue.

While my name goes on the cover, all books are made by a gang of people who do various bits of work you never notice. Mary Treseler, my editor and friend, who greenlights these crazy ideas I have for books and wisely guides their way, simply rocks. O'Reilly Media needs to clone this woman. My friend, Marlowe Shaeffer, who has worked, mostly voluntarily (firearms were only involved twice, fired once), on all my books at O'Reilly. Also a candidate for cloning. Rob Romano rocked with the illustrations, Angela Howard crushed the index, Ron Bilodeau made the insides all nice and cool, Monica Kamsvaag made the unmistakable cover, and production editor Rachel Monaghan shepherded all these diverse talents together to create a single bound object worthy of your hard-earned cash. And thanks to Christine Walker, Sara Peyton, and all my friends at O'Reilly Media for helping promote this thing.

To the Donner party (Terrel Lefferts, Rob Lefferts, Kaelyn Lefferts, Oliver Lefferts, Royal Winchester, Andrea Winchester, Skaeya Winchester, and Jill Stutzman) for collectively restoring my faith in humanity.

For giving various honest and possibly intoxicated opinions, digging up facts beyond my reach, or providing otherwise generous positive support for my work (listed in a secret order I will never reveal): Richard Grudman, Chris McGee, Jeffrey Bialy, Bob Baxley, Bob Sutton, Jeff Veen, Russ Miles, Fitz, Kim Ricketts, Mary Treseler, Terrel Lefferts, Rob Lefferts, Neil Enns, Brady Forrest, Chris Baty, Jared Spool, Dana Chisnell, Pam Daghlian, Royal Winchester, Andrea Winchester, Vanessa Longacre-Wilcox, Lauren Cramer, Jeff Veen, Ron Fein, Eugenio Perea (@eperea), Kaleem Khan (@kaleemux), Sarah Milstein, Lynn Cherny, Todd Berkun, Sarah Davies, and Brian Rowe.

I'd like to say hi to everyone who didn't answer my email. Hi. Your name could have been here.

For my regular haunts where much thinking on this book was done: Blue Ginger (Bellevue), Crossroads (Bellevue), Pho Than Brothers (Redmond), Half Price Books (Redmond), the Seattle Public Library, and the King County Metro 545 express bus that takes me there.

To Groucho, the crazy owl who hoots at 2 a.m. outside my window, reminding me I'm not the only fool awake and working.

For photographic consultation: James Duncan Davidson, Randy Stewart, Del Paquette, Neil Enns, and Shawn Murphy.

Thanks to Beth Goldman and Mary Duffy at CNBC and Stu Hitchner at Fisher Pathways studios for photo permissions and general coolness.

To Bryan Zug, Brian Dorsey, and Stewart Maxwell, for the pho-laden lunch conversation that helped me rewrite Chapter 1.

To the teachers who changed my life and inexplicably set a time bomb for making me want to teach: Alan Stein (Bayside High School), Todd Berkun, Jerry Reinstein (Bayside High School), Don Cole (Drew University), and Willfred Seig (Carnegie Mellon University).

Love, but also anti-thanks, to Bonnie Sheehan, Ryan Grimm (who drinks lesbian beer for its urbane and discriminating flavors), and Jason Hunter for stealing my Moleskine at FOO and watching me look for it like an idiot for 20 minutes. Lesson: never fuck with a writer. We will write about you. :)

If you saw someone you know in here, please say hi to them for me.

Peanut M&Ms consumed during writing of this book: 12,428

Regular M&Ms consumed: 65

Number of regular M&Ms confused with peanut M&Ms: 65

Bowls of pho eaten: 105

Moleskines filled: 3

Games of *Gears of War 2* (Horde) played: 168

Number of bowls of pho confused with peanut M&Ms: 0

Knees sprained: 2

Point per game average before knee sprain / after: 16.2 / 1.4

Progress of human race: not verified, but technically possible

Planets destroyed: 0

Universes experienced: 1

Paradoxes solved: unknown

Music listened to: Aimee Mann, Cat Power, Bon Iver, The Avett Brothers, Patty Griffin, The Frames, Charles Mingus, The Breeders, Duran Duran, Bruce Springsteen, Elliott Smith, Cake, Rilo Kiley, Paul Simon, The Pretenders, The Clash, The Pixies, Flogging Molly, The Pogues, Social Distortion, Johnny Cash, Eddie Vedder (*Into the Wild* soundtrack), They Might Be Giants, Mozart, Bach, Bob Dylan, Bell X1, Woody Guthrie, Billy Bragg (*Mermaid Avenue*), Sufjan Stevens, Rufus Wainwright, PJ Harvey, Palomar, DeVotchKa, Beethoven, and the great Sonny Rollins.

# Photo credits

All photos used by permission and listed in order of appearance. Thanks to everyone for allowing me to use their work.

**Chapter 1**

Opener, P.S. Zollo (& JP) (*http://www.flickr.com/photos/zollo/404871195/*)

Figure 1-1. James Duncan Davidson, Scott Berkun at Web 2.0 Expo

**Chapter 2**

Opener, Terri Fisher (*http://www.flickr.com/photos/fish747/240988262/*)

Figure 2-1. Scott Berkun, Audience, RIM; Robin Drucker Photography, Lion, Auckland, New Zealand (*http://www.flickr.com/photos/lightknight/495334127/*)

**Chapter 3**

Opener, Dennis Mojado (*http://www.flickr.com/photos/refractedmoments/223052548/*)

Figure 3-1. Josh Evnin, Ft. Mason, San Francisco, California (*http://www.flickr.com/photos/jevnin/60967651/*)

Figure 3-2. Scott Berkun, National War Museum, Kiev, Ukraine

**Chapter 4**

Opener, Steve Rhodes (*http://www.flickr.com/photos/ari/450369238/*)

Figure 4-1. Randy Stewart, Berkun in relief, King Kat Theater, Seattle, Washington

Figure 4-2. Jason Morrison (*http://www.flickr.com/photos/jason-morrison/928112787/*)

Figure 4-3. Paul Gould, Adamson Wing, Carnegie Mellon University, Pittsburgh, Pennsylvania

**Chapter 5**

Opener,     Shaun     Bromley     (*http://www.flickr.com/photos/barrowfordred/2729402584/*)

Figure 5-1. Ted Leung, Scott Berkun at Ignite! Seattle, Seattle, Washington

**Photos you don't expect to see**

Scott Berkun, Scott miserable in Vancouver International Airport

Neil Enns/Dane Creek Photography, Lectern at Microsoft, Redmond, Washington

Kevin Fox, Architecture tour, New York City, New York

Shawn Murphy, Scott in background, Redmond, Washington

Jean-Jacques Halans, Scott at Web Directions 2007, Sydney, Australia

Randy Stewart, Scott at Ignite! Seattle, Seattle, Washington

Scott Berkun and Randy Stewart (image at bottom right), Six venues

**Chapter 6**

Opener, Vince Hrabosky (*http://www.flickr.com/photos/kitsu/404092967/*)

**Chapter 7**

Opener, Vicki Huckle (*http://www.flickr.com/photos/toria_77/3839065689/*)

Figure 7-1. Captured from CNBC, *The Business of Innovation*

Figure 7-2. Scott Berkun at CNBC Studios, photo by permission

Figure 7-3. Captured from CNBC, *The Business of Innovation*

Figure 7-4. Scott Berkun (Taken at Fisher Pathways studios, Seattle, Washington)

Figure 7-5. Scott Berkun (Taken at Fisher Pathways studios, Seattle, Washington)

Figure 7-6. Scott Berkun at CNBC Studios, photo by permission

## Chapter 8

Opener, Alan Strakey (*http://www.flickr.com/photos/smoovey/3297533849/*)

## Chapter 9

Opener, Pierre-Alexandre Pheulpin (*http://www.flickr.com/photos/pierre-alexandre/3561333458/*)

## Chapter 10

Opener, Nicky Werner (*http://www.flickr.com/photos/andersdenkend/1429241231/*)

## Backstage notes

Opener, Del Paquette, at T4G innovation day, Toronto Science Center

Figure A-1. Shawn Murphy, Confidence monitor, at Microsoft Corporation, Redmond, Washington

Figure A-2. Scott Berkun, Logitech Presenter

Figure A-3. Neil Enns/Dane Creek Photography, Stack of books, Redmond, Washington

All other photos by Scott Berkun

# Index

# About the author

Scott Berkun is the bestselling author of *The Myths of Innovation* and *Making Things Happen* (both O'Reilly). He worked at Microsoft from 1994–2003, mostly as a program manager for Internet Explorer 1.0 to 5.0, quitting in 2003 with the goal of filling this shelf with books he's written. If he were smarter, he would have picked a smaller shelf.

His work as a writer and public speaker have appeared in the *Washington Post, New York Times, Wired, Fast Company, Forbes,* and other media. He has taught creative thinking at the University of Washington, and has been a regular commentator on CNBC, MSNBC, and NPR.

His many popular essays and entertaining lectures can be found for free on his blog at *www.scottberkun.com*. If you want to hire him to speak at an event, teach a workshop, or be your personal speaking coach, head over there.

# Colophon

The cover image is a composite of two photos from iStock and Corbis. The cover font is ITC Franklin Gothic. The text font is Sabon; the heading font is BentonSans. The paper for these fine pages is 50-pound Crème, a perfect blend of moderate porosity (air permeability of less than 15 centimeters per minute), delightful compressibility, and high-performance ink hold-out ratios, well suited for confessional and memoir monographs.

And thus, in a few simple sentences, you have now read the greatest, most miraculous colophon of all time.

You see, what you can't possibly know is that once upon a time, one score and 17 years ago, in a galaxy not at all far away, on a planet indistinguishable from the one you are on now, it was a dark time for colophons. Few knew what colophons were for, nor who wrote them. Billions of people finished books every year, denied the sacred knowledge of what kind of paper had been in their hands and what typefaces they'd read, and fell into suicidal levels of depression. It was a dark time indeed.

But that year something happened. The greatest colophonist of all time was born. Her powers were so far beyond mortal comprehension, they called her the chosen one.

She could identify fonts in 6-point type, while blindfolded and standing on one foot, from several hundred miles away. With barely a sniff from her perfect little nose, she could name the inks used on even the oldest pages known to man. With the slightest touch of her pinkie finger, and the thinnest slice of attention from her potent mind, she could sense the weight of any print stock made, and the genus and species of all trees used to produce them.

Her only aids were a small set of magical colophony tools she'd forged from metals too rare to be known to ordinary men, tools she kept in a small satchel. A satchel she kept safe by strapping it to her foot. Legend has it, this sacred satchel was called, to those permitted to say the words, the *divine footbag*.

But since her natural powers were unmatched and her force of mind incomparable, she rarely used those tools nor opened the sacred bag on her foot that contained them.

To our great sadness, for years she refused to work on any books, feeling they were unworthy of her world-transforming powers. She wrote colophons in private and kept them for herself. There were rumors she'd ghostwritten colophons for J. D. Salinger and Thomas Pynchon, but those rumors were never confirmed.

When she was asked to work on this book, the world shook at the prospect that she might say yes. Angels cried in joy. Writers considered being less pretentious. Politicians wondered about committing fewer crimes. Even the rain made plans to avoid weddings and camping trips forevermore. It was a wondrous moment of potential for life, the universe, and everything.

But she said no.

She found us and our ways quite annoying.

Especially our tendency to use single-sentence paragraphs.

And the world wept.

Twice.

And when we did not give up, instead choosing to hound her relentlessly to work on this book through emails, text messages, and boxes of homemade cupcakes that said, in 6-point Arial vanilla micro-frosting we knew only she could read, "Pleeeeze be our colofoonist!", she became angry. She knew Arial was a font for lazy heathens, a disrespect to her talents and her kind. Hell hath no fury like a colophonist scorned. All too late we realized our mistake, and knew the next time she saw us, it would be the end of us all.

The next day, as we stumbled in misery through town, knowing all was lost without a good colophonist for this book, we saw her across the street, and she saw us, too. We considered running, but there was nowhere to hide. Her eyes narrowed intensely, in the same terrifying way they did when she found a mislabeled typeface or poorly sourced cover stock photo. She pounced off the sidewalk and raced into the street at preternatural speed and at an angle that defied the laws of geometry, making our escape impossible. But we did not despair, for she made one mistake. She forgot to look both ways before crossing. And she was crushed by the oncoming bus.

It was in fact two buses, one going in each direction, but the effect on her powers was much the same. The buses—with large advertisements well labeled in 80-point Helvetica heavy bold, printed on prepressed sheets of four-color vinyl, produced by a digital printscreen transfer—flattened her like an *escalope*. Her wondrous powers were no more.

Emerging from the carnage, bouncing and rolling its way to our feet, was a small satchel. Could it be? Yes, indeed. It was the small magic bag she wore on her foot. The footbag had survived. Behold the mighty footbag!

And it was only through the careful application of those tools, tools not meant for mere mortals to see, much less use, that the immense challenges of this colophon were overcome. If it were not for the sacrifice of the chosen one, this colophon, this book, and this entire publishing industry we take for granted would not have been possible. Instead of the glory of this colophon and its related—possibly fictional—backstory, this page would be empty and you'd forever wonder about the making of the book you just read. May the footbag, and the wonders of colophons, stay with us forever. Long live the colophon.

This page has intentionally not been left blank.

But there's nothing to see here. Please move along.

Really. We're all finished now. Don't you have friends to talk to or places to go? There must be something better to do with your time than look for strange messages on what should be a blank page.

OK, I have one last confession.

All your base are belong to us.

# Get even more for your money.

## Join the O'Reilly Community, and register the O'Reilly books you own. It's free, and you'll get:

- 40% upgrade offer on O'Reilly books
- Membership discounts on books and events
- Free lifetime updates to electronic formats of books
- Multiple ebook formats, DRM FREE
- Participation in the O'Reilly community
- Newsletters
- Account management
- 100% Satisfaction Guarantee

### Registering your books is easy:
1. Go to: oreilly.com/go/register
2. Create an O'Reilly login.
3. Provide your address.
4. Register your books.

Note: English-language books only

**To order books online:**
oreilly.com/order_new

**For questions about products or an order:**
orders@oreilly.com

**To sign up to get topic-specific email announcements and/or news about upcoming books, conferences, special offers, and new technologies:**
elists@oreilly.com

**For technical questions about book content:**
booktech@oreilly.com

**To submit new book proposals to our editors:**
proposals@oreilly.com

**Many O'Reilly books are available in PDF and several ebook formats. For more information:**
oreilly.com/ebooks

# O'REILLY®

Spreading the knowledge of innovators                    oreilly.com

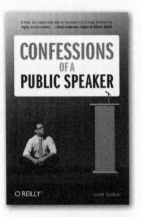